He's a butler whose job is being unlucky.

HAYATE THE COMBAT BUTLER
VOL. 8

STORY AND ART BY
KENJIRO HATA

English Adaptation/Mark Giambruno
Translation/Yuki Yoshioka & Cindy H. Yamauchi
Touch-up Art & Lettering/Freeman Wong
Design/Yukiko Whitley
Editor/Kit Fox

Editor in Chief, Books/Alvin Lu
Editor in Chief, Magazines/Marc Weidenbaum
VP of Publishing Licensing/Rika Inouye
VP of Sales/Gonzalo Ferreyra
Sr. VP of Marketing/Liza Coppola
Publisher/Hyoe Narita

Printed in Canada

Published by VIZ Media, LLC
P.O. Box 77010
San Francisco, CA 94107

10 9 8 7 6 5 4 3 2 1
First printing, August 2008

store.viz.com

VIZ
MEDIA
www.viz.com

Hayate
the Combat Butler

Wataru Tachibana

Registration for Admission Documents

Hakuou Gakuin
Admissions Exam Center

KENJIRO HATA

Contents

Sept. 18th

By Class President-san ♡

Episode 1
"Good, or Don't Be"
5

Episode 2
"Your Place"
21

Episode 3
"Nagi's Angels: Full Throttle"
37

Episode 4
"*Elevator Action* Was Beyond the Comprehension of
Those of Us Who Couldn't Become Newtypes"
53

Episode 5
"Struggling with Jealousy!! Ja-pan"
69

Episode 6
"Running to Horizon"
85

Episode 7
"Round Dance—Revolution—"
101

Episode 8
"Why Do I Always Watch *Princess Mononoke* on TV? I Own It on DVD…"
117

Episode 9
"Project Isumi ~ The Challengers ~ Tonight's Story Is
About Ambitious Girls in Skirts"
133

Episode 10
"*Please Save My Earth* with a 130 cm Dandy, Darling"
149

Episode 11
"I Used to Think That It Was Normal to Fish Like the Crazy Old Men of the Sea"
165

Episode 1:
"Good, or Don't Be"

GLOOM

...SUCH AN IDIOT...

I AM...

...KISSED HIM...

...K...

I EVEN...

...BUT HAD HIM DRY MY HAIR...

I NOT ONLY LET HIM SEE ME NAKED...

RUB RUB

KISS

...THAT I WON'T BE ABLE TO FACE HAYATE FOR A WHILE...

NGHAAA!!

THIS IS SO EMBAR-RASSING...

BLUSH

...COULD YOU PLEASE STAY SOME- WHERE ELSE FOR A BIT?

...AND SO, HAYATE- KUN...

WELL, IT SOUNDS LIKE THAT MIGHT BE BEST...

HA HA ...

EH? IS THAT OKAY?

...PLEASE STAY AT A HOTEL AND ENJOY YOURSELF.

ANYWAY, I'M GIVING YOU A FEW DAYS OFF UNTIL NAGI CALMS DOWN, SO...

KLAK KLAK

BEEP BEEP

OH, NO. I DON'T MIND...

I'M SORRY THAT BECAUSE OF NAGI YOU HAVE TO...

...THIS SHOULD COVER EXPENSES FOR A THREE- NIGHT STAY...

SHFF

IT'S NOT MUCH, BUT FOR THE MOMENT...

YES.

MARIA-SAN!! TH...TH... THIS IS **ONE MILLION YEN*!! A MILLION!!**

EHH ...?!

...

* about $9,600

I MEAN, WITH A MILLION YEN, SOMEONE COULD LIVE FOR MORE THAN *THREE MONTHS!* In my case, it would last three years!!

NO, NO!! I DON'T NEED THIS MUCH FOR THREE DAYS!!

IF YOU RUN OUT, PLEASE LET ME KNOW. I'LL GIVE YOU SOME MORE...

A MILLION YEN FOR THREE DAYS... THEIR FEELINGS TOWARDS MONEY ARE UNBELIEVABLE...

THEY'RE WEALTHY, ALL RIGHT...

EH? EHH?! ARE... ARE YOU SURE?!

WELL, IT WOULD COMPLICATE THINGS TO RETURN IT, SO JUST BE SURE TO SPEND IT ALL.

IS THAT SO?

I NEED TO SPEND IT *WISELY!!*

BUT, JUST BECAUSE I WAS GIVEN A LARGE SUM OF MONEY, I SHOULDN'T SQUANDER IT...

IT'S UNUSUAL TO SEE YOU IN REGULAR CLOTHES!!

OH!! AYASAKI-KUN!!

HM? ME?

IT'S...IT'S NOTHING...SAY, IT'S UNUSUAL TO SEE YOU AROUND HERE, SENSEI. WHAT ARE YOU UP TO RIGHT NOW?

WHY DID SOMEONE WHO LOVES TO SQUANDER MONEY SHOW UP OUT OF THE BLUE?

UDA5AN

BA-DUMP, BA-DUMP

WHA—?! WHY ARE YOU PUTTING UP YOUR GUARD ALL OF A SUDDEN?

FSST

W-WELL, I'M BROKE TOO, SO EXCUSE ME...

TURN

MY INSTINCTS ARE TELLING ME NOT TO GET INVOLVED!!

AS I SUSPECTED, SHE'S COMPLETELY HOPE-LESS!

I WAS SORT OF WONDERING IF SOMEONE COULD LEND ME SOME MONEY...

WELL... I'M BROKE AND I'M ABOUT TO BE THROWN OUT OF THE NIGHT-DUTY ROOM...

Tee hee

9

HELLO, HOW HAVE YOU BEEN?

HIMURO-SAN... WHY ARE YOU HERE ALL ALONE?

GAH!!

I SOMEHOW SENSE THE PRESENCE OF MONEY...

EH? YOU'RE JOKING!! SERIOUSLY?!

WELL, THE **MONEY RADAR** IN MY HEAD IS TELLING ME THERE'S CASH AROUND HERE.

BUT, HIMURO-SAN... W-WHAT DID YOU MEAN ABOUT FEELING THE PRESENCE OF MONEY?

DAMN IT!! HOW COULD HE DETECT THAT?!

THERE'S A MILLION YEN INSIDE YOUR POCKET.

THERE'S NO WAY A POOR PERSON LIKE ME WOULD HAVE ANYTHING TO DO WITH A LARGE SUM OF MONEY...

NO... YOU'VE GOT TO BE KIDDING, HIMURO-SAN...

YOU'RE KIDDING!! FOR REAL?! HAVE YOU REALLY GOT A MILLION IN CASH, AYASAKI-KUN?!

I MEAN... WOULD YOU HAPPEN TO POSSESS ONE MILLION YEN, AYASAKI-*SAN*?!

WHAT'S WITH THE SUDDEN USE OF HONORIFICS?!

I'M NOT GOING TO GIVE IT TO YOU EVEN IF YOU *BEG* FOR IT!! NOT THIS!!

SHE'S TRYING TO HUSTLE ME NOW?!

AYASAKI-KUN, WHY DON'T YOU JOIN ME?!

BY THE WAY, I SUDDENLY FEEL LIKE PLAYING *MAHJONG* ...

ARE YOU SURE?!

WE'RE NOT ROBBERS, YOU KNOW.

OH... OH, NO. I WOULDN'T TRY TO GET MONEY FROM ONE OF MY STUDENTS.

THIS IS A *SHŌNEN MANGA*, SO THERE'S NO WAY WE'D BET MONEY ON MAHJONG!!

IT'S OKAY!! WHAT ARE YOU WORRIED ABOUT?!

BESIDES, THAT'S A CRIME!!

NO, THANKS!! I DON'T BET ON MAHJONG!!

...BUT PLAYING WITH THREE WOULDN'T BE VERY INTERESTING...

I'D PLAY A LITTLE IF WE HAD FOUR PEOPLE...

YES. I'M TOTALLY FINE WITH NOT BETTING ANY MONEY.

AH!! GOOD TIMING, SISTER!! DO YOU KNOW HOW TO PLAY MAHJONG?

AW, DOUBLE DAMN IT!!

DIVINE GUIDANCE MUST HAVE LED ME HERE...

...

DENTAL CLINIC

FUJII BENTO MEGUMI

...WHY DON'T YOU PLAY WITH US A WHILE?

WELL, TO STRENGTHEN OUR *BONDS OF FRIENDSHIP*...

I'M SO GLAD...♡ SO, NOW THAT WE HAVE FOUR PLAYERS...

ALL RIGHT.

IF THAT'S THE CASE...

BUT I DON'T THINK I'LL LOSE AT MAHJONG, SINCE I WAS A MAHJONG DAIICHI* AT THE AGE OF 13..!

WHEN IT COMES TO MONEY, I CAN'T USE PHYSICAL FORCE TO DEFEAT THEM. IT'S NOT EVEN EASY TO ESCAPE...!

DAMN... KATSURA-SENSEI, HIMURO-SAN AND SISTER...

*A player who acts something like a bodyguard, pitting his skills against Yakuza-types that threaten places such as mahjong parlors.

SOUNDS GOOD!!

BUT I'M ONLY PLAYING *ONE* GAME.

FORTY PU, THREE HAN. THAT'S 5,200 POINTS, AYASAKI-KUN.

TAN-YAO TOI TOI.

RON!!

TAK

BUT...

THESE THREE...

I'M LOSING? THIS CAN'T BE HAPPENING...

HA HA, YOU MUST HAVE SOME CONFIDENCE IN YOUR ABILITIES SINCE YOU WERE A DAIUCHI AT 13, BUT...

...ARE FIERCE!!

BUT THEY'RE COUNTING ME AS ONE OF THEM! EVEN THOUGH I'M PERFECTLY NORMAL!!

URGH...NOW I GET IT. CLEARLY, NONE OF THEM HAVE LED WHAT COULD BE CONFUSED AS AN "AVERAGE" LIFE...

...WHO'S LED SUCH A DANGEROUS LIFESTYLE.

...YOU'D BE WRONG TO THINK YOU'RE THE ONLY ONE...

HM? WHERE ARE YOU GOING?

SHFF

I SEE. IF THAT'S THE CASE, I AM GOING TO GET SERIOUS!!

I'M GOING TO **CRUSH** ALL OF YOU!!

GLARE

ALL OF YOU ...

DON'T WORRY, I'M NOT GOING TO RUN AWAY.

TO THE REST-ROOM. I'M GOING TO CLEAR MY HEAD.

WELL ...

TOILE[

...

FWUP

...I LEFT BEHIND MY COAT AND 50,000 YEN... MEANING I HAVE 950,000 YEN LEFT...

BUT... SO AS NOT TO LET HIMURO-SAN AND THE OTHERS KNOW...

SHF

I'D BETTER RUN AWAY...

LONG TIME NO SEE...

HEYYY! HAYATE-JAN.

...I HAVE TO SPEND THE REST VERY WISELY...

THAT WAS QUITE AN UN-EXPECTED EXPENSE, SO...

SEE YA!! BE SURE TO CALL US SOME-TIME!!

AH!! ME, TOO!!

AH!! SHOOT, I'LL BE LATE FOR MY PART-TIME JOB!!

EXCUSE ME. PLEASE BRING US FIVE MORE CHOCOLATE PARFAITS!!

BLAH BLAH YAMMER

...

SO... HOW YOU BEEN? YOU LOOK PALE...

...I STILL HAVE MORE THAN 900,000 YEN, SO...

WELL...THAT WAS AN UN-EXPECTED EXPENSE AT AN UNEXPECTED PLACE, BUT...

OH... I'LL PAY FOR IT.

UMM... I DON'T HAVE ANY MONEY...

...

...AND SPEND THE REST OF MY TIME QUIETLY!!

...I SHOULD JUST CHECK INTO A HOTEL RIGHT AWAY...

I TOLD YOU, *I DON'T CARE!!*

BUT IF YOU TAKE THAT 500,000 YEN BACK, MY DAUGHTER'S LIFE WILL—

...

Ehh...

WHAM

WHAM

WHAM

SO PAY THE MONEY BACK *RIGHT NOW!!*

HEY, HEY!! WE DON'T GIVE A DAMN ABOUT YOUR SICK DAUGHTER'S MEDICAL BILLS!!

THERE'S NO ONE WHO WOULD HELP...

AT ANY RATE, THERE'S NO END TO HELPING PEOPLE LIKE THAT...

IT'S NONE OF MY BUSINESS... NONE...

SO? IT'S NOT OUR PROBLEM !!

PLEASE!! THAT'S JUST WHAT WE NEED SAVE OUR DAUGHTER!!

NO ONE WOULD HELP...

16

UM...

YES ...

R-REALLY ?!

YOU ...

UMM... I COULD LEND YOU THE 500,000 YEN...

YOU'RE... AYASAKI ...

...OJÔ-SAMA MAY SCOLD ME...

YES, BUT... IF I PRETEND NOT TO NOTICE THIS...

ISN'T THAT RATHER NAIVE?

COVERING SOMEONE ELSE'S DEBT, JUST BECAUSE SOMEONE PAID YOURS...

SIGH ...

FOR SOME REASON, TODAY WAS A TOTAL WASH-OUT...

SHUFFLE

It's cold...

NO, NO ...

IN OTHER WORDS, HE'S STUPID AND HAS A LOLITA COMPLEX.

OJÔ-SAMA? DOES HE MEAN THAT LITTLE GIRL FROM BEFORE?

WITH THAT MUCH, I SHOULD BE ABLE TO STAY AT MOST OF THE HOTELS IN TOKYO...

OH WELL, I STILL HAVE MORE THAN 400,000 YEN!!

CRASH

AH!! I-I'M SORRY!!

BECAUSE YOU STOPPED SO SUDDENLY... THE PRECIOUS VASE MY MOM ASKED ME TO GO BUY IS...

...

HUH?

AREN'T YOUR EXPECTATIONS A BIT HIGH FOR THIS BOY'S FIRST ERRAND?

MADAM!!

THAT ARITA-YAKI SOMENISHIKI VASE WAS WORTH 400,000 YEN!!

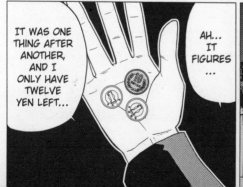

IT WAS ONE THING AFTER ANOTHER, AND I ONLY HAVE TWELVE YEN LEFT...

AH... IT FIGURES...

AND SO...

LOSER PARK

HOW COULD I TELL HER THAT I LOST A MILLION YEN IN ONE DAY!!

HOW COULD I?!

IF YOU RUN OUT, PLEASE LET ME KNOW.

SERIOUSLY, THIS IS THE PITS...

FEBRUARY IS ALMOST OVER, BUT IT'S SNOWING...

AH... WHY AM I ALWAYS LIKE THIS?

WELL, THE DIFFERENCE IS...THIS TIME, IT'S MY OWN FAULT, AND...

THIS IS A BIT LIKE THAT CHRISTMAS NIGHT...

SHFF

!

...TO SAVE ME...

...THERE'S NO OJÔ-SAMA...

WHAT ARE YOU DOING HERE, AYASAKI-KUN?

HINAGIKU-SAN...

...

YOU'LL CATCH COLD IF YOU STAY HERE LIKE THAT.

...ON THE NIGHT IT SNOWED FOR THE LAST TIME THAT WINTER.

♪ HUH?

...COME OVER TO MY PLACE?

ANYWAY, YOU LOOK COLD...DO YOU WANT TO...

IT HAPPENED...

Episode 2: "Your Place"

PLIP

...BATHES HERSELF EVERY DAY...

AND THIS IS WHERE HINAGIKU-SAN...

YOU FOOL!! WHAT ARE YOU THINKING?!

SPLASH SPLASH

UWAAAH!!

BOYS SURE TAKE SHORT BATHS. LIKE "A CROW TAKING A QUICK DIP," THEY SAY.

Y-YES...

DID IT WARM YOU UP A BIT?

OH? DONE WITH YOUR BATH ALREADY?

ARE MY HUSBAND'S CLOTHES TOO BIG FOR YOU?

AH, AYASAKI-KUN, ARE YOU DONE WITH YOUR BATH?

AREN'T YOU A LITTLE OLD TO GET THAT EXCITED?

?

WHISPER WHISPER WHISPER

WELL... HE SURE IS A CUTIE... ♡

REALLY? I'M GLAD...

NO, THEY'RE FINE...

I ALREADY SAID HE WASN'T!!

ARE YOU SURE HE ISN'T YOUR BOYFRIEND OR SOMETHING? I'D BE TOTALLY FINE WITH SOMEONE THAT CUTE BECOMING MY SON-IN-LAW. ♡

?

?

I TOLD YOU TO STOP DOING THAT!!

I'M QUITE SURE HE'D LOOK GOOD IN IT.

HEY, HEY, IS IT ALL RIGHT TO DRESS HIM UP IN HINA-CHAN'S SKIRT?

...A GIRL-FRIEND ALREADY...

BESIDES, AYASAKI-KUN PROBABLY HAS...

...HINAGIKU-SAN...

AND I WAS FOUND BY:..

MORE THINGS HAPPENED, AND THE ONE MILLION YEN MARIA-SAN HAD GIVEN ME FOR LODGING EXPENSES WAS GONE...

A LOT OF THINGS HAPPENED, AND I HAD TO STAY AWAY FROM THE MANSION FOR THREE DAYS...

WHY AM I IN THIS SITUA-TION?

BY THE WAY...

...I'VE BECOME A GOOD-FOR-NOTHING MAN WITH NO PLACE TO CALL HOME...

AH, I SEE. I JUST REALIZED THAT ONCE AGAIN...

UH!! UM!!

I'D BE HAPPY TO STAY AT HINAGIKU-SAN'S PLACE LIKE THIS, BUT... I CAN'T ASK HER FOR A FAVOR THAT BIG...

AUGH!! B-BECAUSE...

GEEZ!! WHY ARE YOU ASKING SUCH EMBARRASSING THINGS?!

HUH?

WOULD YOU... WEAR THEM?

T-THESE ARE **CAT EARS**...

EH? IS... IS THAT OKAY WITH YOU?

YOU'RE STAYING FOR DINNER, RIGHT?! I HAVEN'T EATEN YET, EITHER!!

GEEZ!! THIS WAY, AYASAKI-KUN!!

NO... THAT'S ALL RIGHT...

CLATTER PSSSH CLATTER

SHE GETS EXCITED WHEN SHE SEES BOYS LIKE AYASAKI-KUN...

I'M SORRY.

...

PSSSH

...AND VERY KIND.

BUT YOUR MOTHER IS FUNNY...

26

? SHE'S VERY KIND.

YEAH.

BECAUSE I HAD NO MONEY AND NO PLACE TO GO AND WAS LOOKING FOR SOME-PLACE I COULD STAY FOR FREE...

AH...

UM... UM...

HEH?

BUT...WHAT WERE YOU DOING OUT IN THE SNOW, WEARING ONLY A T-SHIRT?

I CAN'T GO BACK FOR ABOUT THREE DAYS...

UM...

EH? IS THAT RIGHT?

!!

Urgh!!

DON'T TELL ME YOU COULDN'T GO BACK TO NAGI'S?

I MEAN, IT'S ALREADY LATE AND IT'S COLD OUTSIDE, SO JUST STAY OVER!!

WELL, WOULD YOU LIKE TO STAY OVER?!

OF COURSE, IT'S **TOTALLY** ALL RIGHT!!

IT'S ALL RIGHT!!

B-BUT IS THAT REALLY ALL RIGHT?

OKAY?! OKAY?!

UH... UMM...

You have an adolescent daughter in the house...

...

THERE'S A ROOM IN THE GUEST COTTAGE MY OLDER SISTER ISN'T USING, SO YOU CAN HAVE THAT!!

I'LL SHOW YOU TO YOUR ROOM!!

Eager

ALSO, I HAVE A FRILLY DRESS HERE THAT HINA-CHAN REFUSES TO WEAR...

Eager

KA-CHAK

...

Hina-chan is so mean...

Sniff

SHE WAS BEING A BOTHER, GETTING DRUNK BY HERSELF EVERY NIGHT, SO I KICKED HER OUT.

IT'S LITTERED WITH LIQUOR BOTTLES...

IT'S MESSY, BUT ONEE-CHAN WON'T BE BACK, SO MAKE YOURSELF AT HOME.

UWAH.

AH, YES...

ANYWAY, I'LL COME SEE YOU LATER.

AND, THERE'S SOMETHING I WANTED TO ASK YOU...

WE SHOULD ALL HELP EACH OTHER IN TIMES OF NEED.

EITHER WAY, SORRY I JUST HAPPENED TO SHOW UP LIKE THIS.

I WONDER WHAT SHE'S DOING RIGHT NOW...

OJÔ-SAMA...

...BUT HINAGIKU-SAN'S PLACE IS PRETTY BIG...

IT'S NOT LIKE THE SANZENIN FAMILY MANSION...

KLAK

...THIS MANSION FEELS REALLY *BIG*...

WITH-OUT HAYATE...

JUST GIVE HIM A CALL AND HAYATE-KUN WILL HAPPILY RETURN.

IF YOU'RE LONELY, WHY DON'T YOU HAVE HIM COME BACK?

I WONDER IF I WILL GET USED TO ITS SIZE SOME-DAY...

THIS MANSION WAS BIG FROM THE START.

NO, NO. THIS ISN'T LIKE NOBITA'S HOUSE...

I HOPE HAYATE-KUN DOESN'T CATCH COLD OR SOME-THING.

THERE ARE THINGS I CAN AND CAN'T DO IN SUCH SHORT TIME. MY HEART CAN'T BE REPAIRED OVERNIGHT.

I...I CAN'T DO THAT.

353...

PRESS

352...

NGH NGH NGH

357...

356...

354...
355...

SO YOU *DO* TRAIN HARD AFTER ALL...

WOW...

I SEE. WELL, I'M COMING IN.

YES, I DO... THIS HAS BEEN MY DAILY ROUTINE SINCE I WAS LITTLE...

DO YOU DO THAT EVERY DAY?

UWAH!! HINAGIKU-SAN!!

OH... THANKS.

AH, THIS IS FOR YOU.

BUT IF YOU SWEAT LIKE THAT, DOESN'T IT FEEL UNCOMFORT-ABLE IF YOU DON'T TAKE A BATH AFTER-WARDS?

YOU'RE REALLY DEDICATED...

OH, YOU WERE STUDYING.

...JUST BATHED...

...HINAGIKU-SAN...

IT LOOKS LIKE...

HEY, YOU!!

...HEY.

TH-THIS IS...

IN A CLOSED ROOM... LATE AT NIGHT... JUST THE TWO OF US, THE VERY DELICATE SCENT OF HER SHAMPOO...

BA-DUMP BA-DUMP BA-DUMP   BA-DUMP BA-DUMP

HUH ?!

YOU MADE A MISTAKE HERE.

BUT... I'VE BEEN THINKING ABOUT IT FOR A WHILE NOW...

AH... THIS IS WRONG, TOO...

O-OF COURSE !!

ARE YOU LISTENING TO ME?

WHAT DO YOU MEAN, "HUH"?

AFTER ALL, HINAGIKU-SAN IS...

...A BEAUTIFUL GIRL...

To solve this problem, first...

UWAAH!!

PAT

...I'M GOING TO BLUSH...

N-NO!! IF I THINK ABOUT IT TOO MUCH...

...SO YOU HAVE TO WORK ON THIS EQUATION...

...

Pure Sake

Fragile!

EH?

W-WHAT WAS IT?

B-BY THE WAY, HINAGIKU-SAN, YOU SAID YOU HAD SOMETHING TO ASK ME?

S-SORRY!! I'M SORRY!!

HELLO? WOULD YOU MIND LISTENING TO ME?

RIGHT... THAT'S... WELL...

AH...

Y-YES!!

I'LL TUTOR YOU, SO GET TO WORK RIGHT NOW!!

AH?! R-RIGHT!!

NEVER MIND. WHAT ARE YOU GOING TO DO ABOUT THE NEXT EXAM IF YOU KEEP MAKING SO MANY MISTAKES?

WHAT I WANTED TO ASK HIM WAS...

UHH...

UMM...

WHAT I WANTED TO ASK...

...ARE YOU GOING OUT WITH HER, HAYATE?

RIGHT NOW...

FOR THAT GIRL WHO CONFESSED TO LOOK SO HAPPY MUST MEAN...

AND MEAN... I'M HERE TO THANK YOU FOR THAT, BUT...

Y... YES!!

WERE YOU ABLE TO CONVEY YOUR FEELINGS...

...ABOUT THAT VALEN- TINE'S DAY...

WHAT WOULD I DO AFTER ASKING HIM THAT?

OH, COME ON!!

34

HINAGIKU-SAN IS TAKING SPECIAL TIME TO TUTOR ME!!

I HAVE TO DO MY BEST!!

EH?

NEVER MIND...

...

UM, I'M DONE... HOW DOES IT LOOK?

...

GOOD NIGHT.

THIS WAS *POINT-LESS*, AFTER ALL...

Sigh

...THAT BAD?

IS MY WORK ...

NNGH...

NGH...

CHIRP CHIRP CHIRP

OKAY.

WOULD YOU WAKE UP AYASAKI-KUN?

HINA-CHAAAN...

WELL... BECAUSE MY WORK WAS...

OH? WHY WERE YOU UP ALL NIGHT, STUDYING?

MISUNDER-STANDINGS CAN ARISE FROM VERY TRIVIAL THINGS.

HEY, AYASAKI-KUN.

BREAK-FAST IS READY...

Episode 3:
"Nagi's Angels: Full Throttle"

THE MISUNDERSTANDING WAS INEVITABLE.

AND SO... I'M HERE TO THANK YOU FOR THAT, BUT...

Y.... YES!!

...THE GIRL ANSWERED WITH A SMILE...

WERE YOU ABLE TO CONVEY YOUR FEELINGS?

BE- CAUSE...

...WHEN SHE ASKED *THAT*...

ME TOO, HONEY. I'VE ALWAYS LOVED YOU WITH ALL MY HEART.

I LOVE YOU, HAYATE- KUN.

NATU- RALLY...

...IT WAS ALMOST CUSTOMARY TO IMAGINE A SITUATION SUCH AS THIS.

THIS IMAGINARY LOVE SCENE BROUGHT TO YOU COURTESY OF THE HAKUOU GAKUIN STUDENT BODY PRESIDENT'S SUBCONSCIOUS.

WHA—?! WHO YOU ARE CALLING *LAME*?!

COULD A PLOT DEVELOP- MENT BE ANY *LAMER*?

WHO WOULD'VE KNOWN THAT EVEN THOUGH SHE'D CONFESSED, SHE HAD YET TO RECEIVE ANY CLOSURE ON THE ISSUE...

YOU DON'T NEED...

...TO GIVE ME AN ANSWER...

IN THE FIRST PLACE, IT'S NONE OF MY CONCERN WHO AYASAKI-KUN GOES OUT WITH.

WHY SHOULD I BE SO FLUSTERED ABOUT THIS?!

...THE GIRL'S STATE OF MIND WAS TROUBLED.

THAT WAS WHY, A WEEK AFTER VALENTINE'S DAY...

I DON'T CARE ABOUT HIM...

IT'S NOT LIKE HE'S MY TYPE OR ANYTHING.

THERE'S...

...REALLY NOTHING TO IT...

...WHEN SOMEONE THEY KNOW FINDS A BOYFRIEND...

SO, THIS IS JUST THE WAY A PERSON FEELS...

WOW...

AND NOW, THE PERSON WHO THE GIRL AGONIZED OVER FOR ONE LONG WEEK IS...

CHIRP

...IS SO TASTY...

SMILE

THE BREAKFAST HINAGIKU-SAN MADE...

...AWAKENS MURDEROUS INTENT INSIDE OF ME?

...LOOKING AT THAT CAREFREE SMILE...

I WONDER WHY...

NOT REALLY. DO YOU WANT SECONDS? THERE'S STILL A LOT LEFT.

UMM... HINAGIKU-SAN? DID I DO SOMETHING WRONG?

?

SERIOUSLY... HE HAS NO IDEA HOW I FEEL...

AH... IF THAT'S THE CASE...

BY THE WAY, AYASAKI-KUN...

...IT COULD MEAN TROUBLE IN A LOT OF WAYS...

...IF I DON'T UNCOVER THE CAUSE QUICKLY...

WHAT'S GOING ON? I DON'T UNDERSTAND, BUT...

AH...IF IT'S NOT GOING TO TROUBLE YOU... UM...

NOD NOD

IT APPEARS THIS PERSON WANTS YOU TO STAY OVER, TOO.

IF YOU DON'T HAVE A PLACE TO STAY, YOU COULD SLEEP HERE AGAIN.

WHAT ARE YOU GOING TO DO ABOUT TONIGHT?

IS IT ALL RIGHT TO NEGLECT YOUR SWEETHEART (NISHIZAWA-SAN)?

WELL... UMM...

HUH? WHAT DO YOU MEAN?

IT'S NO TROUBLE FOR US, BUT...IS IT REALLY ALL RIGHT?

(SHE'S EMBARRASSED ABOUT BEING SEEN IN THE NUDE) AND AS A MAN, I DON'T THINK I SHOULD PESTER HER TOO MUCH.

WELL, SHE (OJŌ-SAMA)... NEEDS TO BE LEFT ALONE FOR A WHILE, YOU SEE...

OF COURSE. I KNOW WHAT I'M DOING.

YOU SEEM TO HAVE THOUGHT ALL THIS OUT.

NOW THAT SHE'S CONFESSED, IS HE GIVING HER THE COLD SHOULDER ON PURPOSE?

AH, DON'T WORRY ABOUT THAT.

WHAT ARE YOU GOING TO DO ABOUT YOUR CLOTHES? IT'S IN-APPROPRIATE TO WEAR STREET CLOTHES.

BUT WE HAVE TO GO TO SCHOOL TODAY.

DON'T HIDE STUFF LIKE THAT IN THE STUDENT BODY ROOM, OKAY?

...SO I HID A SPARE BUTLER UNIFORM AND A SCHOOL UNIFORM HERE.

I THOUGHT SOME-THING LIKE THIS MIGHT HAPPEN...

KLAK

...SO PLEASE DON'T PEEK.

W-WELL, I'M GOING TO CHANGE...

HOW DARE YOU SUGGEST I'D *PEEK!*

!!!

Augh !!

BA- DUMP

WHAT'S THIS EROTIC GAME CALLED?

STRIPPING DOWN IN THE STUDENT BODY ROOM SO EARLY IN THE MORNING...

Geez

MORNING, HINA.

MIKI... YOU'RE RATHER EARLY TODAY.

WHY AM I HERE? BECAUSE I HAVE SOME STUDENT BODY BUSINESS TO ATTEND TO.

H-HANA-BISHI-SAN!! W-WHY...

O-OF COURSE NOT!!

Whisper Whisper

Mutter Mutter

LISTEN!! DON'T TELL **ANYONE** THAT YOU'RE STAYING OVER AT MY PLACE!!

HUH ?!

TH-THAT'S NOT TRUE!!

BUT THIS IS QUITE UN-EXPECTED. IT'S STILL MORNING AND YOU TWO SEEM TO BE VERY CLOSE.

NOTHING AT ALL!!

N-NOTHING!!

WHAT?

AH, ALL RIGHT.

FWIP FWIP

OKAY. I'LL WORK ON IT RIGHT NOW, SO YOU TWO GO ON AHEAD TO CLASS.

OH, IT'S DUE TODAY.

Graduation Ceremony

BY THE WAY, HINA, HERE'S WHAT WE TALKED ABOUT DOING YESTERDAY.

I SEE. NEVER MIND, THEN.

AH...IT'S NOTHING IMPORTANT, BUT...

WHAT'S WRONG?

...

44

...I JUST THINK IT'S AMAZING HOW QUICKLY SHE CAN SWITCH INTO FULL STUDENT BODY PRESIDENT MODE...

GIVEN HOW SHE WAS A MOMENT AGO...

NOW THAT YOU MENTION IT, OJŌ-SAMA ONCE TOLD ME THAT THERE WAS A STUDENT WHO SKIPPED GRADES AT AN AMAZING RATE AND SERVED TWO CONSECUTIVE TERMS...

WOW, IS THAT SO?

...WHO BECAME HAKUOU STUDENT BODY PRESIDENT IN THEIR FIRST YEAR.

OBVIOUSLY, SHE'S AMAZING. INCLUDING HINA, THERE ARE ONLY TWO PEOPLE...

...CAN SERVE AS HAKUOU STUDENT BODY PRESIDENT.

SO ONLY THOSE WHO ARE TRULY GIFTED...

THAT'S RIGHT, JUST HINA AND THAT GIRL GENIUS.

ACHOO

I JUST HAD AN ITCHY NOSE.

NO...

DID YOU CATCH A COLD?

WHAT'S WRONG, MARIA?

OH, A GUEST?

DING DONG

WHA—?! WHO ARE YOU CALLING **WEAK**?!

TRUE GENIUSES DON'T GO EASY ON THE WEAK. ♡

TRAIN YOUR BRAIN! TRAINING FOR CHILDREN

I SEE. BUT I WON'T BE ABLE TO WIN IF YOU DON'T GO EASY ON ME.

IT'S A LONG STORY. THERE WAS SOME MONEY INSIDE, SO I THOUGHT I SHOULD BRING IT OVER.

OH, KATSURA SENSEI... HOW DID YOU GET THIS?

THANK YOU FOR WAITING.

WELCOME.

AYASAKI-KUN FORGOT THIS.

HERE.

AH... YES.

WELL, EITHER WAY, PLEASE GIVE IT TO AYASAKI-KUN...

YEAH...I WAS UP ALL NIGHT BECAUSE OF HAYATE-KUN.

Ahh, I'm really late...

YOU SEEM VERY TIRED.

EXCUSE ME...

...50,000 YEN?

INSIDE IT WAS...

...A PERSON BY THE NAME OF HAYATE AYASAKI-SAN HERE?

Wow... a maid

Sure is...

IS THERE ...

THEY RETURNED 999,988 YEN, WHICH IS ALMOST ONE MILLION YEN.

THAT'S THE AMOUNT I GAVE HAYATE-KUN YESTERDAY FOR LODGING EXPENSES...

OH, IT'S NOT A BIG DEAL, BUT...

WHAT'S WITH THE LOOSE CHANGE?

...I WONDER WHERE HAYATE-KUN IS STAYING?

WHICH MEANS...

UH-HUH. BUT WHY AREN'T YOU WEARING YOUR BUTLER'S UNIFORM?

Y-YOU THINK SO?

YOU LOOK GOOD IN A SCHOOL UNIFORM TOO, HAYATA-KUN.

WOW...

I DON'T WANT HER TO PRY TOO MUCH AND FIND OUT THAT I'M STAYING AT HINAGIKU-SAN'S PLACE...

AH... WELL... THAT'S...

AH, HELLO, THIS IS AYASAKI.

HUH?

HM? HAYATA-KUN, YOU HAVE A PHONE CALL...

I'D GET BUSTED FOR LOSING ONE MILLION YEN IN A SINGLE DAY... ESPECIALLY IF MARIA-SAN FINDS OUT...

BEEP BEEP

K...LAK

EH?! MARIA-SAN?!

BA-DUMP

AH, HAYATE-KUN. I HAVE SOMETHING TO ASK YOU...

...

TRRR TRRR

BIP★

OH!! MY CLASS IS GOING TO START... AH...

AH!! I'M SORRY. SEEMS LIKE I'M GETTING A WEAK SIGNAL HERE!!

UM...

I SHOULD USE THAT METHOD TO CHECK ON HIM.

SO...

HE'S AT SCHOOL RIGHT NOW...

...ANOTHER DISASTER GATHERING SPEED...

CHING

THIS... SEEMS TO BE...

THIS WAY I CAN SECRETLY OBSERVE HAYATE-KUN.

YES, YES... THIS IS PERFECT.

...I STILL LOOK PRETTY GOOD IN IT, DON'T I?

I'll just...

...spin around a bit. ♥

EVEN THOUGH IT'S BEEN A WHILE SINCE I WORE THIS SCHOOL UNIFORM...

COMPARED TO THOSE DAYS, I MAY LOOK EVEN BETTER IN IT NOW...

IT'S TRUE THAT I SERVED AS STUDENT BODY PRESIDENT STARTING IN MY FRESHMAN YEAR, BUT I WAS ONLY 10 YEARS OLD BACK THEN...

WHAT'S WITH THE WEIRD COSPLAY?

MARIA...

Shiver   Shiver

ANYWAY, I'M GOING OUT TO TAKE CARE OF SOME BUSINESS!!

B-BUT...

W-WHAT COSPLAY?!

IN THE NEXT EPISODE, AN EARLY (OR IS IT LATE?) SPRING STORM HITS HAKUOU GAKUIN!!

...and stuck at home...

I'm all alone...

UH... I JUST HAD A BAD PREMONI- TION...

WHAT'S WRONG, HAYATA- KUN?

A CHOO

52

Episode 4:
"*Elevator Action* Was Beyond the Comprehension of Those of Us Who Couldn't Become Newtypes"

BRING ME SOME TEA...

HEY, MARIA...

...

...WAS BUILT SO THAT ONLY MARIA, HAYATE AND KLAUS COULD COME IN CONTACT WITH HER.

BECAUSE NAGI HATED HAVING SERVANTS AROUND...

...THE MAIN BUILDING OF THIS MANSION...

HAYATE ISN'T HERE, AND MARIA WENT OUT, SO SHE'S NOT HERE EITHER...

OH... R-RIGHT...

SILENCE

...

H-HEY... MARIA...

Maria...

Calling out to her once more, just in case.

Y-YEAH...

THAT CONFIRMS SHE'S NOT HERE...

Just casually turning up the volume on the TV.

BEEP BEEP BEEP

I SURE WISH SHE WOULD COME BACK SOON...

Giving up...

Para-normal sound.

KRAAK

BA-DUMP

...BREW SOME TEA...

...I COULD...

ALL BY MY-SELF...

Just singing out her thoughts.

55

MEANWHILE, THE MAID IN QUESTION...

MURMUR

...WAS AT HAKUOU GAKUIN TO LOOK FOR HAYATE, WHO'D BEEN ACTING STRANGELY.

MURMUR
MURMUR
MURMUR

COULD SHE BE A TRANSFER STUDENT?

NO...

Whisper
Whisper

WAS THERE A PRETTY GIRL LIKE THAT AT THIS SCHOOL BEFORE?

I...I DON'T KNOW.

Whisper

HEY... WHO'S THAT CUTE GIRL?

URGH...

...

...

Mutter ...
Mutter ...

Pss Pss

...LOOK FOR HAYATE-KUN **DISCREETLY**...

I WORE THIS UNIFORM IN ORDER TO...

...I'M ATTRACTING ATTENTION...

BUT FOR SOME REASON...

I HAVEN'T WORN THIS IN A WHILE, SO I WONDER IF SOMETHING'S OUT OF PLACE?

WHY IS THAT?

WORRY

WORRY

FWUP

FWUP

AH. ♡ I KNOW WHAT TO DO.

SPARKLE SPARKLE

USING GLASSES AS A DISGUISE...

Nice...

MURMUR

Oh...

...HAD THE OPPOSITE EFFECT...

NOW WHAT DO I DO?

URGH...

BUT THAT WASN'T THE RIGHT THING TO DO...

I HUNG UP ON MARIA-SAN AFTER MAKING SOME CHILDISH EXCUSES...

URGH...

MEANWHILE, OUR HERO WAS ALSO EXPERIENCING VARIOUS PROBLEMS.

YES, I'M SORRY.

OH, YOU SPENT THE ONE MILLION YEN?

IF I TOLD HER THE TRUTH...

...I PROBABLY DIDN'T NEED TO LIE IN THE FIRST PLACE...

AFTER ALL, WITH MARIA-SAN...

THAT'S RIGHT!! THE SITUATION COULD DEVELOP THAT WAY, AND...

WOW, THANK YOU.

...BUT BE KIND TO OTHERS IN MODERATION, OKAY? ♡

WELL, I'LL GIVE YOU ANOTHER MILLION YEN...

...I HAVE NO CHOICE BUT TO LIE...

LISTEN!! DON'T TELL ANYONE THAT YOU'RE STAYING OVER AT MY PLACE!!

THAT'S RIGHT... SINCE I CAN'T TELL HER THAT I STAYED AT HINAGIKU-SAN'S PLACE...

URGH!!

SO? WHERE DID YOU STAY LAST NIGHT?

I'M SUCH A HOPELESS HUMAN BEING...

SIGH...

COMPOUNDING LIES...

HERE, TAKE THIS.

WHEN YOU LOOK DULL, YOUR LIFE BECOMES DULL.

HINA-GIKU-SAN.

HYAAA!!

WHY DO YOU LOOK SO DE-PRESSED?

PAT

YOU ALREADY HAVE A FACE THAT ATTRACTS MISFORTUNE.

YOU SHOULDN'T LOOK SO DEPRESSED.

AH, THANK YOU VERY MUCH.

...

...SO DRINK THAT AND CHEER UP.

WELL, I STILL HAVE STUDENT BODY DUTIES TO ATTEND TO...

I SHOULD... TRY TO HELP HINAGIKU-SAN A BIT WITH HER WORK...

JUST STAYING AT HER PLACE WITHOUT CONTRIBUTING ANYTHING ISN'T RIGHT...

HMMMM...

NOW I LOOK LIKE AN ORDINARY FEMALE STUDENT IN EVERY WAY.

NOTE: THIS IS MARIA.

GLEAM

THESE ARE PERFECT.

...

WELL... I SHOULD GO LOOK FOR HAYATE-KUN RIGHT AWAY...

...I MIGHT AS WELL GO UP.

AS LONG AS I'M HERE...

...SURE BRINGS BACK MEMORIES.

THE CLOCK TOWER...

SKCH

COINCIDENCE

EH?

AH...

...

H-HAYATE-KUN...

AH...

...RECOGNIZE ME?

DOESN'T HE...

HUH?

UM... YOU'RE GOING UP, RIGHT? WHICH FLOOR?

SHE IS A DIFFERENT PERSON, JUST AS I THOUGHT.

AH, YES.

UH... THE TOP FLOOR...

...MARIA-SAN WOULDN'T COME HERE, ESPECIALLY DRESSED LIKE THAT. SHE HAS TO BE... SOMEONE ELSE...

I THOUGHT SHE WAS MARIA-SAN FOR A MOMENT, BUT...

↖Uh, inside the elevator?

...WANT TO PLAY A LITTLE TRICK...

IT MAKES ME...

...THAT HE DIDN'T RECOGNIZE ME...

BUT... IT'S A BIT AMUSING...

NO... I'M NOT...

HUH?

UM... ARE YOU A MEMBER OF THE STUDENT COUNCIL?

REALLY?

SO I THOUGHT I SHOULD HELP HER OUT...

UM...THE STUDENT BODY PRESIDENT IS SORT OF TAKING CARE OF ME...

EH? AH... THAT'S TRUE, BUT...

OH? I THOUGHT ONLY MEMBERS OF THE STUDENT COUNCIL WERE ALLOWED TO ENTER...

KACK

BY ANY CHANCE, ARE YOU *IN LOVE* WITH THE STUDENT BODY PRESIDENT?

WELL, NATURALLY, I FIND HER ATTRACTIVE, BUT...THAT'S... THAT'S NOTHING LIKE BEING IN LOVE...

Panic Panic

UM...SHE'S COOL AND BEAUTIFUL AND THERE'S NO REASON TO DISLIKE HER...

IT... IT'S NOT LIKE THAT!!

EH? DENYING IT SO STRONGLY MAKES ME WONDER EVEN MORE...

WHA... WHA...?! WHAT MAKES YOU SAY SOMETHING LIKE THAT?!

WOW...

...

SO... UMM... UH...

UM...

...WANT TO TEASE HIM EVEN MORE...

LET'S JUST SAY THAT MAKES ME...

HAYATE-KUN... YOU'RE SO CUTE...

EH?

CLUNK

HM? OH?

LET'S SEE, WHEN IT STOPS...

BEEP BEEP.

AHHH... THIS ELEVATOR IS OLD, SO IT STOPS SOME- TIMES...

SHUUU

OH? DID IT STOP?

...MARIA- SAN AFTER ALL?

IS SHE REALLY ...

I SHOULD MAKE A STRAIGHT- FORWARD APOLOGY...

THIS... THIS ISN'T GOOD...

DID SHE COME TO CHECK UP ON ME IN PERSON BECAUSE I HUNG UP ON HER? OR MAYBE SHE CAME TO SCOLD ME?

EH? BUT WHY?

65

JUST BECAUSE WE'RE ALONE, HAYATE-KUN CAN'T BE THINKING OF...

EH? WH-WHAT'S THIS ABOUT?

KYA!!

EXCUSE ME!!

GNNN

GNNN

CLUNK

WHOA!!

KYA!!

WHUMP

I'M SORRY THIS IS SO SUDDEN!! BUT, YOU SEE...

NO, NOT LIKE THIS!!

GNNN

GNNN

AH...

Y-YES... WHAT IS IT?

UH... UM, MARIA-SAN...

WOULD YOU LISTEN TO ME CALMLY?

IS EVERYONE INSIDE ALL RIGHT?

IT'S FIXED.

GRNNG

EH?

WHAT ARE YOU DOING, AYASAKI-KUN?

WHA—?

EH?

UM... HAYATE-KUN, WHAT WERE YOU GOING TO TELL ME?

I'D LIKE TO TELL HINAGIKU-SAN THAT "THIS HAPPENED WHILE TRYING TO APOLOGIZE TO MARIA-SAN," BUT IT'S IMPOSSIBLE TO EXPLAIN THAT WITHOUT MENTIONING THE MILLION YEN... UMM...IF THAT'S THE CASE...

...

IF I TELL MARIA-SAN THAT I LOST ONE MILLION YEN... SHE'LL ASK ME WHERE I STAYED LAST NIGHT...

THIS DOESN'T SOUND LIKE A *JOKE* TO ME.

SINCE THIS IS AN ELEVATOR, HOW ABOUT A PUNCH LINE LIKE, "WE FELL *DOWN* ON THE WAY *UP*"...?

...

P S S H

GRNNG

only trying to brew some tea...

was...

NO... THAT'S NOT WHAT I'M ASKING ...

WELL, LET ME EXPLAIN... THE JOKE WAS THAT WE WERE KNOCKED "DOWN" TO THE FLOOR AS THE ELEVATOR WAS GOING "UP," SO...

COME BACK HERE!!

WHA—?! WAIT, AYASAKI-KUN!!

Episode 5:
"Struggling with
Jealousy!! Ja-pan"

...

DISASTER AREA

Smolder...

...

IT'D BE EASIER IF HAYATE-KUN WERE HERE...

SHE DID ALL THIS IN JUST THREE HOURS?

Is she a kitten or something?

YES... I KNOW...

I WAS... I WAS JUST TRYING TO BREW MYSELF SOME TEA!!

IT'S... IT'S NOT WHAT YOU THINK!!

CLATTER

70

...WHERE HAYATE-KUN IS STAYING...

I FORGOT TO ASK...

AH... THAT REMINDS ME...

SO... WHY ARE YOU HERE AT HAKUOU, MARIA-SAN?

DING DONG

ABOUT AN HOUR AGO...

HE LOOKED OKAY, SO I DON'T NEED TO WORRY...

BUT, WELL...

S-SORRY. MARIA-SAN. YOU'RE VERY MATURE, SO...

Without thinking...

GEEZ... BOTH YOU AND NAGI...

IF YOU TAKE INTO ACCOUNT THE FACT THAT I'M 17, IT'S ONLY NATURAL!!

THIS ISN'T COSPLAY!!

AND WHY ARE YOU C-COS-PLAYING?

It seems almost criminal...

AS I THOUGHT, IT'S BECAUSE I HUNG UP ON HER...

EH?

HAYATE-KUN... YOU REALLY HAVE NO IDEA?

SO... MARIA-SAN, WHY ARE YOU HERE...?

At Hakuou...

...BECAUSE I WAS WORRIED!

HAYATE-KUN, I CAME HERE...

BA-DUMP BA-DUMP

THAT'S WHY SHE GOT ANGRY... AND...

...

THAT'S RIGHT.

YOU WERE WORRIED... ABOUT ME?

...I THOUGHT YOU WERE SHORT ON MONEY, SO I CAME HERE.

YOU'RE FINALLY TAKING SOME TIME OFF, HAYATE-KUN, BUT...

HUH?

Sigh...

...

AS A MATTER OF FACT, THE MONEY I GAVE YOU WAS...

PLIP PLIP

...MARIA-SAN WORRIED ABOUT ME AND...

I'VE NEVER HAD ANYONE WORRY ABOUT ME LIKE THAT, AND...

It made me happy, so...

UH... BECAUSE... BECAUSE ...

WAAH!! WHAT ARE YOU CRYING ABOUT, HAYATE-KUN?!

PU-RU-RU-RU-RU

SO HAYATE-KUN, ARE YOU—

THERE WAS NO MALICIOUS INTENT THERE, RIGHT?

NO MALICIOUS INTENT...

...HAD TO DRESS UP IN SUCH *EMBARRASSING* CLOTHES...

DON'T WORRY. I WON'T WORRY YOU ANY MORE, MARIA-SAN!!

UM... HAYATE-KUN, I HAVE TO...

HUH? THE ROOM IS A MESS?

I...I SEE! I'LL BE RIGHT BACK!!

AH... NAGI? WHAT IS IT?

YES?

JUST BECAUSE I HAD A DAY OFF, I'D GOTTEN TOO RELAXED...

ROGER!!

DASH

...PLEASE COME BACK TOMORROW NIGHT, OKAY?

W-WELL THEN, HAYATE-KUN...

...I REMAIN A SANZENIN FAMILY BUTLER!!

AT ALL TIMES...

TOK TOK

SHFF

I'M HAPPY THAT MARIA-SAN WAS WORRIED ABOUT ME, BUT...

...I SHOULDN'T MAKE HER WORRY LIKE THIS AGAIN...

...IS A DISGRACE TO ALL OF BUTLERDOM!!

IT APPEARS HE GETS FIRED UP WHEN WEARING THESE CLOTHES.

IN THAT CASE, BEING CARED FOR AT HINAGIKU-SAN'S PLACE FOR FREE...

DOOM

OH, YOU'D LIKE TO HELP ME?

SPARKLE SPARKLE SPARKLE

...COULD YOU PREPARE HINA'S DINNER?

WELL, SINCE I WAS CALLED IN UN-EXPECTEDLY FOR THE NIGHT SHIFT...

THE BEAUTY PARLOR... It can change a woman that much?

OH, YOU NOTICED?

HAVE YOU CHANGED YOUR LOOK, MA'AM?

UH... UMM...

I WENT TO THE BEAUTY PARLOR.

Tee-Hee

...WITH A DIFFERENT GIRL...

HE HAS A GIRLFRIEND, YET HE DOES SOMETHING LIKE THAT...

GNNN GNNN

...IT SEEMS LIKE HE COULD BE A WOMAN-IZER...

HE MAY NOT LOOK IT, BUT...

SERIOUSLY... HOW COULD AYASAKI-KUN DO THAT?

SHUFFLE

...SO COULD YOU PREPARE SOMETHING FOR BOTH OF THEM?

YUKI-CHAN SHOULD BE BACK BY EARLY EVENING...

YES!! LEAVE IT TO ME!!

OTHERWISE, I'LL BRING SHAME UPON THE OFFICE OF HAKUOU STUDENT BODY PRESIDENT!!

IF SO, THEN BECAUSE HE'S STAYING AT MY PLACE... I SHOULD GIVE IT TO HIM STRAIGHT...

ARE YOU HEADED HOME NOW? YOU MUST BE TIRED.

URGH...! AYASAKI-KUN!!

AH, HELLO, HINAGIKU-SAN.

BARGAIN SALE

LETTUCE

110!

VEGETABLES

THEN WHAT ABOUT FOODS YOU LIKE?

L-LET'S SEE... PICKLED JAPANESE PLUMS... I DON'T CARE FOR THINGS THAT ARE REALLY SOUR...

ERMARKET

YES.

HUH? FOOD I DON'T LIKE?

BY THE WAY, HINAGIKU-SAN, IS THERE ANY KIND OF FOOD YOU DON'T LIKE?

AYASAKI-KUN, YOU—

? ... YES. HUH? FOODS I LIKE?

...HAM-BURGER... C-CURRY AND...

WHY ARE YOU ASKING QUESTIONS LIKE THAT?

AH!! LIKE, WHAT'S WITH YOU?!

WHA... WHAT?! THERE'S NOTHING WRONG WITH THAT! BOTH CURRY AND HAMBURGER ARE TASTY!!

HA HA, YOU SEEM TO LIKE THE KIND OF FOOD THAT BOYS PREFER.

YES. YOUR MOTHER TOLD ME THAT SHE HAD TO WORK THE NIGHT SHIFT.

EH? DOES THAT MEAN...

OH, YOUR MOTHER ASKED ME TO PREPARE DINNER AND I THOUGHT I'D BETTER COOK SOMETHING HINAGIKU-SAN WOULD LIKE...

WHA—?! WHAT?! WHAT DO YOU MEAN BY *THAT*?!

WELL, I DON'T THINK THERE'S ANYONE BRAVE ENOUGH TO TRY SOMETHING JUST BECAUSE THEY'RE ALONE WITH YOU, HINAGIKU-SAN.

NO... SHE SAID KATSURA SENSEI WILL BE COMING OVER IN THE EVENING.

EH? DOES THAT MEAN WE'RE GOING TO BE ALONE?

TH-THAT'S NOT TRUE!! I JUST WANT TO ENJOY THE TRUE ESSENCE OF CURRY!!

YOUR TASTES ARE UNEXPECTEDLY SIMILAR TO THOSE OF A YOUNG CHILD.

AH!! NO, YOU HAVE TO GET THAT MILDER CURRY SAUCE OVER THERE!!

HOW... HOW RUDE!!

BECAUSE IF HE TRIED ANYTHING, HE WOULD PROBABLY GET BEATEN DOWN BY A WOODEN SWORD...

NEW PRODUCT SALE

SALE 99.

IF I DON'T DO SOMETHING, I'M GOING TO CONTINUE GETTING TRIPPED UP BY AYASAKI-KUN.

SERIOUS-LY...

DAMN!! WHAT'S WITH THE "CHUMMY HIGH SCHOOL KIDS" TALK?!

THERE WAS NO ONE NEARBY TO BUTT IN ON YOUR BEHALF, SO I HAD THE FLOOR MANAGER (SINGLE, AGE 42) AT THE SUPER-MARKET DO IT.

OKAY, OKAY, HINAGIKU-SAN. ♡

GEEZ!! LET'S JUST GO HOME, AYASAKI-KUN!!

78

IF THAT'S THE CASE...

...

...I HAVE TO GIVE IT TO HIM STRAIGHT...

For the dignity of the Student Body President...

SOMEHOW, BEFORE ONEE-CHAN COMES HOME...

SHFF

BOTH DISHES SEEM SIMPLE, YET PROFOUND...

CURRY AND HAMBURGER...

SO I'M GOING TO HELP YOU!!

I CAN'T STAND BY AND JUST LET YOU COOK FOR ME...

EH? HINAGIKU-SAN?!

WAIT, AYASAKI-KUN!!

...I AM GOING TO PREPARE THE **ULTIMATE CURRY AND HAMBURGER** USING EVERY TECHNIQUE I HAVE!!

BUT AS A SANZENIN FAMILY BUTLER...

SHF

DID I SAY IT HAD TO BE A MATCH?

AH!! ALL RIGHT!! IT'S A COOKING BATTLE SIMILAR TO A MIXED MARTIAL ARTS MATCH, BUT...I'LL ACCEPT YOUR CHALLENGE!!

WHY DON'T WE JUST SPLIT IT? AYASAKI-KUN HANDLES THE CURRY AND I'LL WORK ON THE HAMBURGER!!

IT'S OKAY!!

EH? BUT ...

AH... YES ...

AYASAKI-KUN, CUT THE VEGETABLES OVER ON THAT SIDE!! I'M GOING TO PREPARE THE HAMBURGER ON THIS SIDE!!

WHAT ARE YOU TALKING ABOUT?! LOOK HERE!!

OH, IT'S NOT? I ASSUMED THAT SINCE YOU'RE SOMEONE WHO HATES TO LOSE...

DAMN!! WHAT'S WITH THE "NEWLY-WED COUPLE" TALK?!

DON'T BE SILLY. OH, COULD YOU HAND ME THE CARROTS OVER THERE?

WOW, YOU'RE GOOD AT SLICING ONIONS, HINAGIKU-SAN.

OKAY.

THERE WAS NO ONE NEARBY TO BUTT IN ON YOUR BEHALF, SO I HAD THE DOVE (COMMON DOVE, AGE 3) DO IT.

COO COO

OF COURSE!! HOW LONG ARE YOU GOING TO KEEP TREATING ME LIKE A CHILD?!

HINAGIKU-SAN, DO YOU EAT CELERY?

TREMBLE AT ITS AWE-INSPIRING FLAVOR!!

HMPH!! MINE'S READY, TOO!!

WOULD YOU CARE FOR A LITTLE TASTE?

THERE! IT'S READY, HINAGIKU-SAN!!

...

SIP

MUNCH

WOW, THIS IS SO TASTY!!

D-DELICI-OUS!!

SHOCK

SHOCK

ALL THE JUICES HAVE BEEN SEALED IN, SO NONE OF THEM ARE WASTED!!

THE COARSE TEXTURE OF THE MEAT... THE SKILLED KNEADING...

IS THAT FROM THE ONIONS?! AND THE SECRET INGREDIENT IS PINE-APPLE!!

THERE'S A HIDDEN RICHNESS DEEP WITHIN THE SWEET FLAVOR...

...

YOU'RE EMBARRASSED AT HOW YOU'RE ACTING LIKE A LOVING COUPLE!!

YOU GUYS AREN'T EMBARRASSED BY MAKING COMMENTS THAT SOUND BETTER SUITED FOR A COOKING MAGNA!!

THERE WERE NO ANIMALS NEARBY TO BUTT IN ON YOUR BEHALF, SO I HAD THE HOUSEPLANT (CYCAD, AGE 12) DO IT.

SHALL WE SET THE TABLE?

W-WELL...I'M BEGINNING TO GET EMBARRASSED BY MAKING COMMENTS THAT SOUND BETTER SUITED FOR A *COOKING MANGA*, SO...

SILENCE

...

THAT'S TRUE.

HMM... KATSURA SENSEI HASN'T COME HOME YET...

...REALLY GOOD AT COOKING.

AYASAKI-KUN IS...

I WONDER IF HE...

...COOKS FOR HER?

AND THAT DISH...

I COULD TELL JUST BY THE WAY HE MOVES HIS HANDS...

AH, I'LL HELP YOU.

I'M GOING TO BREW SOME TEA.

...

AH...

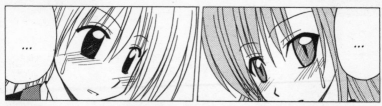

...

...

HMPH!! THERE'S STILL PLENTY OF TIME TILL MORNING!!

LET'S... LET'S PLAY THE NEXT ROUND!!

IT'S SIMPLE *PROBABILITY THEORY.*♡ AT THIS RATE, I'LL BE THE WINNER TONIGHT.

GAH!! HOW COULD YOU PREDICT THAT?!

RON!!

AND, SO... THE NIGHT WITHOUT BUTT-INS CONTINUES.

AH...

N-NO, SAME HERE!!

WHST

WHOA!! S-SORRY!!

AH...

HUH?

IT WAS MY FAULT AS WELL!!

NO... NO!!

IT... IT WAS BEYOND MY CONTROL... NO, I MEAN...

W-WHAT JUST HAPPENED IS, UH...

Episode 6: "Running to Horizon"

Episode 6:
"Running to Horizon"

TICK

TOCK

WELL... UM...

SHE SURE IS...

TICK

TOCK

KATSURA SENSEI SURE IS LATE.

... Ah ha ha...

TICK

TOCK

... Ha ha...

TICK

MUST... FIND... WITTY TOPIC...

I CAN'T KILL TIME THIS WAY...

THIS IS... NOT GOOD...

THIS IS ALL ONEE-CHAN'S FAULT FOR NOT COMING HOME!!

WHY AM I IN THIS SITUATION?

AH, GEEZ...

...ARE THERE ANY ANIME OR MANGA THAT LEFT YOU *FEELING UNSATISFIED*?

AH, BY THE WAY...

ALL RIGHT, I'LL TRY A TOPIC THAT I THINK OJÔ-SAMA WOULD RESPOND TO!!

THAT WAS A TOPIC OJÔ-SAMA AND I COULD HAVE TALKED ABOUT ALL NIGHT LONG!!

AUGH!! HINAGIKU-SAN, YOU SEEM ANGRY FOR SOME REASON!!

SERIOUSLY!! SHE'S REALLY GOING TO GET IT WHEN SHE COMES HOME!!

AZ BL AZ LA ZE BLAZE B

A GIRL-FRIEND...

...

SO... I PROBABLY HAVE NOTHING TO WORRY ABOUT...

NOW THAT I THINK ABOUT IT, AYASAKI-KUN DOES HAVE A GIRL-FRIEND...

EH?

...DO YOU WANT TO TAKE A BATH?

AH, BY THE WAY, AYASAKI-KUN...

ARE YOU KIDDING?

BA-DUMP BA-DUMP BA-DUMP

W-WITH... YOU?

...

...TAKE A BATH WITH ME?

DO YOU WANT TO...

SORRY, I DON'T SPEAK GIBBERISH.

OBO-HEA?!

EHH?! AYA... IAA...

HUH?

...

KAPOK

FSSST

...

IN A CHOICE BETWEEN NISHIZAWA-SAN, MARIA-SAN AND ME, WHO WOULD YOU RATHER TAKE A BATH WITH?

ALL RIGHT, THEN...

90

...

AH... *THAT* IS SOMETHING I WOULD DEFINITELY DECLINE.

What ?! ←That

WELL THEN, WOULD YOU PREFER *MY SISTER?*

I...I MEAN...

N-NO, NO!!

SERIOUSLY...

HMPH...

YOU'RE GOING TO MAKE HER UNHAPPY DOING THAT.

I MEAN... YOU LET YOUR EYES *WANDER,* EVEN THOUGH YOU HAVE A GIRLFRIEND...

...

AYASAKI-KUN, AREN'T YOU BEING A LITTLE TOO FRIVOLOUS?

EH?

I DON'T ...

I DON'T HAVE A GIRL-FRIEND...

UM...

AS I SAID... I DON'T HAVE A GIRL-FRIEND...

...WHAT?

YOU DON'T HAVE A...

EH?

...

AREN'T YOU GOING OUT WITH THAT GIRL, NISHIZAWA-SAN?!

EHH?!

W-W-WHAT MAKES YOU THINK I'M GOING OUT WITH NISHIZAWA-SAN?!

WHAT DO YOU MEAN YOU DON'T HAVE A GIRL-FRIEND?!

HUH?! EH?!

SHE... SHE DID CONFESS, BUT... I HAVEN'T GIVEN HER AN ANSWER YET!!

I *KNOW* SHE CONFESSED HER FEELINGS TO YOU ON VALENTINE'S DAY...

DON'T TRY TO LIE ABOUT IT!!

...

...I COULDN'T GIVE HER AN ANSWER...

SO THAT'S WHY I...

BECAUSE SHE TOLD ME...THAT I DIDN'T NEED TO REPLY RIGHT AWAY...

AND IT WAS JUST A MISUNDER-STANDING ON MY PART... BUT...

EH? SO NOW WHAT? THEY REALLY AREN'T GOING OUT...

?

...AND NOW I'M ALONE WITH A MAN I BROUGHT HERE AT NIGHT...

I BROUGHT A MAN WHO HAS NO GIRL-FRIEND HOME WITH ME...

YES, WHAT IS IT?!

Y-YES?!

UM... HINAGIKU-SAN?

...

HER PERSONALITY IS BASICALLY EARNEST, SO SHE'S BEEN THINKING THAT EVEN THOUGH THEY'RE ALONE, NOTHING WOULD HAPPEN BECAUSE HE ALREADY HAS A GIRLFRIEND.

YEAH!! I'M SURE YOU'D LIKE TO HAVE SOME!! IT SEEMS *REALLY HOT* IN HERE, SO... I'LL GO BUY SOME FOR YOU!!

DON'T YOU FEEL LIKE HAVING SOME *ICE CREAM?*

AH!! SAY, AYASAKI-KUN!!

WELL... UM...

...SHE DOESN'T WANT TO BE ALONE WITH ME?

COULD IT BE...

AH!!

DASH

¥60~

ONIGI

WINE

I NEVER IMAGINED THEY WEREN'T DATING...

HAAH... THAT REALLY THREW ME FOR A LOOP...

Whew

O TASTY!! ODEN

THANK YOU VERY MUCH...

FSSST

...I FELT A LITTLE BIT... UM...

BUT I WONDER WHY...

COINCIDENCE

...

MMF

...

...

NO... MY REASONS ARE NOT THAT AMUSING.

COULD IT BE THAT, LIKE ME, YOU CHASED AFTER A BAKED SWEET POTATO VENDOR, THEN REALIZED YOU'D GOTTEN LOST?

WHY ARE YOU HERE?

Beep Beep

Baked Sweet Potato

Wait!

WHOA!! WHOA!!

YOU'RE THE HAKUOU STUDENT BODY PRESIDENT.

AH!! YOU'RE ...

96

NO, NOT NOW...

AH, WOULD YOU LIKE A BAKED SWEET POTATO?

Baked Sweet Potato

OH... I SEE...

...THAT SHE WAS IN AN EXTREMELY AWKWARD SITUATION.

AT THAT MOMENT, THE THOUGHT THAT FLASHED THROUGH HINAGIKU'S MIND WAS...

IT WAS OBVIOUS THAT, FOR MANY REASONS, SHE WOULD MISINTERPRET THE SITUATION AND MATTERS WOULD BECOME EVEN MORE COMPLICATED!! JUST LIKE A TYPICAL ROMANTIC COMEDY!! THAT'S WHERE THIS IS HEADING!!

?

Mmf Mmf

THE WAY THINGS WERE GOING, NISHIZAWA-SAN MIGHT SOON DISCOVER THAT HAYATE IS STAYING AT HER PLACE...

FOR EXAMPLE, I SHOULDN'T MAKE THE MISTAKE OF DROPPING SOMETHING THAT SHE MIGHT PICK UP LATER, PROMPTING HER TO COME TO MY HOUSE TO RETURN IT, ONLY TO DISCOVER THAT—

I MUST BE CAREFUL NOT TO CAUSE THAT KIND OF MISUNDER-STANDING!!

BA-DUMP BA-DUMP

HE'S HOPELESS, ALL RIGHT.

YOUR BATH IS READY...

AH... HINAGIKU-SAN.

TMP

GACK!!

...

AH... NISHIZAWA-SAN?

HUH?

AYASAKI-KUN!!

DASH

WAIT!!

E-EXCUSE ME!!

N-NO!! IT'S NOT AT ALL WHAT YOU'RE THINKING!!

UMM, UMM...

AH...

HOLD THIS FOR ME!!

FWIP

GEEZ!!

UM...

THE FACT THAT HAYATE-KUN IS STAYING AT THE STUDENT BODY PRESIDENT'S HOUSE MEANS... THEY'RE ALREADY... A NEWLYWED COUPLE!!

I SEE... I DIDN'T KNOW...

HEY!! JUST HOLD ON A MINUTE!!

DASH

...ENGAGING IN AN EXTRA-MARITAL AFFAIR WITHOUT REALIZING IT...

SHE'S CONFUSED, SO SHE'S JUMPING TO CONCLUSIONS.

AND SO, I WAS...

...SHOULD ROT AWAY IN AN UNFAMILIAR TOWN, HOLDING BAKED SWEET POTATOES IN HER HAND!!

IT DOESN'T MATTER!! A GIRL LIKE ME...

BECAUSE YOU'RE RUNNING AWAY!!

WHY ARE YOU CHASING AFTER ME?!

IF THAT'S THE CASE...

GRAB

...THEN WHY DON'T YOU STAY OVER AT *MY PLACE?*

IT'S GOING TO BE A LONG NIGHT.

Two Rons don't make it right!

Ehh?

YEAH. THIS GAME IS *DIVINE.*

I SEE... IS THAT DOGGY THE HERO?

MEAN-WHILE, OUR HEROINES ARE...

...OVER COMPLICATED MISUNDER-STANDINGS...

THAT WAY, YOU WON'T NEED TO AGONIZE...

Episode 7:
"Round Dance –Revolution–"

MEOW☆

BUT...

YOU'RE ASKING ME TO STAY OVERNIGHT AT YOUR PLACE?

B-BUT...

...ISN'T IT?

IT'S BETTER THAN YOU AGONIZING OVER A MISUNDERSTANDING...

...HOW CAN YOU GIVE UP SO EASILY?!

LOOK, IF YOU'RE SERIOUS ABOUT AYASAKI-KUN...

COULD YOU STOP USING SUCH AN OBSCENE EXPRESSION?!

HOW COULD I...STAY IN YOUR "LOVE NEST" WITH HIM?

BA-DUMP

BA-DUMP

AHH!! GEEZ!! DO YOU ALWAYS HAVE TO BE SO CUTE?!

SAYING SUCH THINGS IN FRONT OF THE PERSON IN QUESTION!!

BABBLE BABBLE

WAWA-WAWA!! DON'T!! THAT'S NOT RIGHT, IS IT?

102

OH...

...UNDER THE SAME ROOF OVERNIGHT, YOU SEE...

AND EVEN THOUGH THERE'S NO SPECIAL RELATIONSHIP BETWEEN US... IT'S NOT A GOOD THING TO HAVE AN ADOLESCENT GIRL AND BOY STAYING...

IT WOULDN'T BOTHER ME HAVING A SECOND GUEST.

BUT ARE YOU SURE? ABOUT ME STAYING OVER, THAT IS...

...

WHY SHOULD I...BE... MRFRUBLZ...

O-OF COURSE NOT!!

SO...UM... KATSURA-SAN ISN'T IN LOVE WITH HAYATE-KUN AFTER ALL...

AH, HINAGIKU-SAN, WELCOME HOME...

KA-CHAK

!!

EH?

WHAT SHOULD I DO?

WHA...

...AH!! EHH?!

MEOW

IT WAS DANGEROUS, AND YOU CAN'T ABANDON SOME LITTLE ONE WHO'S LOST HIS PARENTS, RIGHT?!

BUT HE WAS CRYING AND WOULDN'T BUDGE FROM THE MIDDLE OF THE ROAD.

WHAT SHOULD YOU DO?! WHAT HAVE YOU PICKED UP, HINAGIKU-SAN?!

KLAK

FIRST OF ALL, YOU HAVE TO CLEAN HIM UP AND KEEP HIM WARM... A KITTEN CAN'T CONTROL ITS BODY TEMPERATURE YET...

I SEE.

AH, NISHIZAWA-SAN, GOOD EVENING.

Long time no see...

H-hi there.

OH, BY THE WAY, I WAS PICKED UP, TOO.

AHH, WELL, LET ME TAKE HIM.

BEING THAT THIS IS THE FIRST TIME I'VE PICKED UP A KITTEN... WHAT DO I NEED TO DO?

I'M SO GLAD HE'S OKAY.

K-KITTENS ARE SO CUTE, IT'S *CRIMINAL*!!

HE'S SO CUTE!!

PURR PURR

MEOW

WHOOOA!!

HUH?

COME TO THINK OF IT, YOU TWO HAVEN'T SEEN EACH OTHER SINCE VALENTINE'S DAY, HAVE YOU?

OH, I'M JUST USED TO IT...

HAYATE-KUN, YOU KNOW ABOUT A LOT OF THINGS.

THANK YOU, AYASAKI-KUN. I'M GLAD YOU WERE HERE.

VALENTINE'S...

SINCE...

WHY DON'T WE GIVE HIM SOME MILK?

WELL, AT ANY RATE, HE'S STILL A KITTEN ...

... She avoided it...

SHOULDN'T WE FEED HIM?!

AH!! HE'S HUNGRY, DON'T YOU THINK?

MEOW

EH? IS THAT SO?

YOU NEED TO GIVE HIM MILK INTENDED FOR CATS...

AH, YOU SHOULDN'T. REGULAR MILK WILL UPSET HIS STOMACH.

K·LAK

I'LL JUST GO THERE AND BUY SOME SUPPLIES.

PLEASE WAIT. I KNOW A PET SHOP THAT'S OPEN AT THIS HOUR.

EH?

I THOUGHT AYASAKI-KUN WAS *FLAT BROKE*...

YES... BUT...

HAYATE-KUN IS REALLY RELIABLE, ISN'T HE? ♡

SO YOU'RE ASKING ME TO LEND YOU MONEY TO BUY MILK FOR A KITTEN?

SERIOUSLY, I WONDERED WHY YOU CAME OVER IN THE MIDDLE OF THE NIGHT LIKE THIS...

HEY, HEY... ARE YOU JOKING?

ANYWAY, I'LL JUST BUY THIS ONE, AND...

YES, I KNOW, BUT THINGS JUST HAPPENED TO TURN OUT THIS WAY, SO...

THAT'S OKAY, BUT I THINK IT'S A WASTE TO SPEND MONEY ON SAVING A STRAY CAT...

I'M SORRY... I'LL REPAY YOU TOMORROW FOR SURE...

WAKA IS A SERIOUS CAT-LOVER...

AH... R-RIGHT!!

AND JUST IN CASE, YOU SHOULD BUY SOME KITTY LITTER AND THIS TOY, HERE...

He left the shop un-attended

AND YOU'LL NEED THIS LITTLE BABY BOTTLE TO MAKE IT EASIER FOR HIM TO DRINK IT, RIGHT?

HUH?

HE HASN'T BEEN WEANED YET, SO TAKE THIS ONE WITH *LACTO-FERRIN* INSTEAD.

HM? WHAT ABOUT?

WELL, I DO FEEL KINDA RELIEVED.

EH? R-REALLY?!

MY INSTINCTS TELL ME THAT HAYATE-KUN HAS A WEAK SPOT FOR GIRLS LIKE YOU.

AH...

THAT KATSURA-SAN IS NOT IN LOVE WITH HAYATE-KUN OR ANYTHING.

I SEE. BUT, HOW SHOULD I SAY THIS...?

YOU SEE, HE COULD BE MADLY IN LOVE WITH A BEAUTIFUL, KIND AND RELIABLE GIRL LIKE THAT!

THAT'S RIGHT!! BASICALLY, HAYATE-KUN LIKES GIRLS WHO ACT MATURE!!

GEEZ

...

WAWA-WAWA!! L-LIKE I SAID, YOU SHOULDN'T SAY SOMETHING LIKE THAT SO BLUNTLY!!

BUABA!

YOU KNOW SO MUCH ABOUT HIS PREFERENCES, YET FOR YOU TO SAY YOU STILL LIKE HIM MEANS YOU MUST *REALLY* LIKE HIM...

EH?

...MAKES ME WANT TO SUPPORT YOUR EFFORTS.

FOR SOME REASON, SEEING HOW CUTE YOU ARE...

SO I SHOULD...!

THAT'S RIGHT. SHE'S REALLY SERIOUS ABOUT HIM...

NISHIZAWA-SAN?!

SO... UM...

YES.

R-REALLY?

HM? WHY?

BUT...IT COULD BE THAT HAYATE-KUN NEEDS A BACKUP.

I NEVER THOUGHT TO ASK BEFORE, BUT...

COME TO THINK OF IT...

...

...IF HE CAN'T RETURN TO THE MANSION, HE'LL BE OUT ON THE STREETS...

LIKE TODAY... SINCE HAYATE-KUN DOESN'T HAVE A HOME OF HIS OWN...

...AND THEN DISAPPEARED.

HAYATE-KUN'S PARENTS DUMPED THEIR 150 MILLION YEN DEBT ON HIS SHOULDERS...

OH? YOU DIDN'T KNOW, KATSURA-SAN?

WHY IS HE WORKING AS A BUTLER?

WHERE ARE AYASAKI-KUN'S PARENTS?

...

KATSURA-SAN?

SERIOUSLY, I CAN'T BELIEVE SUCH TERRIBLE PARENTS EXIST, BUT...UM...

EH?

...

...BECAUSE I VAGUELY SENSED THAT...

HE PROBABLY CAUGHT MY ATTENTION...

WELCOME HOME.

...AT A GLANCE.

AH, COULD THAT BE HIM?

DING DONG

THERE WAS SOMETHING I COULD SEE...

AH, NISHIZAWA-SAN AND HINAGIKU-SAN... I'M BACK.

...HE MIGHT BE...

...THAT I AM...

?

...FEELING THE SAME PAIN...

...HINAGIKU-SAN...

...

AYASAKI-KUN...

...

KYAA!

UMM... THE KITTEN'S PEEING ALL OVER HIMSELF...

MEOW

PLIP PLIP

AH, SORRY... YOU DIDN'T HAVE TO...

UM, I'LL LEAVE A CHANGE OF CLOTHES HERE.

KA... POK

...

SO IF THERE'S ANYTHING ELSE I CAN DO, PLEASE LET ME KNOW...

I MEAN, IT WAS AWKWARD BEING ALONE WITH HAYATE-KUN...

NO, NO...

...TO YOUR VALENTINE'S DAY CONFESSION?

...DON'T YOU NEED TO KNOW THE ANSWER...

I SEE...

...

IF THAT'S THE CASE...

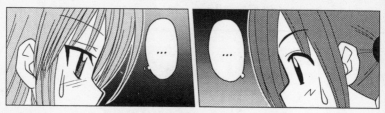

...

...

I KIND OF KNOW THE ANSWER, EVEN WITHOUT ASKING HIM...

HA HA HA

HA HA... THAT'S... UM...

...I'M IN THE MIDDLE OF A POSTPONE-MENT STRATEGY!!

SO AT THIS POINT...

THAT'S...

...EVENTUALLY, THERE MAY BE A CHANCE THAT HAYATE-KUN WILL BE *TEMPTED*, YOU KNOW?

...IF WE CAN STAY TOGETHER FOR A WHILE BY CREATING A RELATIONSHIP WHERE WE'RE MORE THAN FRIENDS BUT LESS THAN LOVERS, THEN...

YOU SEE...

...MY THOUGHTS HAVE BECOME...

THAT'S HOW SHAMELESS...

...

...I WOULDN'T BE TROUBLED LIKE THIS...

IF I COULD BE A COOL GIRL LIKE KATSURA-SAN, THEN...

I'M REALLY...

...NOT COOL AT ALL...

I GET TROUBLED, TOO...

PLIP

...

...I WANT YOU TO CALL ME HINAGIKU...

WE HAVEN'T KNOWN EACH OTHER VERY LONG, BUT...

SHFF

HUH?

...HINAGIKU FROM NOW ON?

HEY... WOULD YOU PLEASE CALL ME...

EH? BUT ...

IS THAT OKAY?

AND IN TURN, I'M GOING TO CALL YOU AYUMU...

SO...

ANYWAY, I ALREADY PROMISED THAT I WOULD BACK YOU UP.

...

WELL... MAYBE IT'S FATE, DON'T YOU THINK?

I ONLY TOLD YOU MY FIRST NAME ONCE...

But you remembered...

...

...THAT'S WHAT I'M GOING TO DO.

WHY ARE YOU ADDING THE HONORIFIC "-SAN"?

That's not fair.

I...I SEE. THEN I'M GOING TO CALL YOU...HIN... HINA-SAN FROM NOW ON...

I STILL AM...

SO YOU'RE NO LONGER EMBARRASSED ABOUT HIM SEEING YOU NAKED?

THAT'S TRUE...

WELL... I'M LOOKING FORWARD TO TOMORROW, KNOWING THAT I'LL GET TO SEE HAYATE.

...THAN HAVING BEEN SEEN... NAKED...

BUT NOT BEING ABLE TO SEE HAYATE'S FACE HAS BECOME MORE OF A BIG DEAL...

...I HOPE YOUR WISH COMES TRUE SOMEDAY...

RIGHT NOW, THAT RELATIONSHIP IS STILL ALL IN YOUR MIND, BUT...

ZZZ

THIS IS GOING TO BE A LONG NIGHT...

YAWN...

YES.

EH? A KITTEN NEEDS TO BE FED MILK EVERY *THREE HOURS?*

LATER...

I'LL... BACK YOU UP.

116

WELL, PLEASE TAKE REALLY GOOD CARE OF HIM, OKAY?

OHHH...

THERE'S NOTHING YOU CAN DO IF YOUR MOTHER IS THAT ALLERGIC TO CATS.

PLEASE DON'T LOOK SO DISAPPOINTED...

I'LL ASK OJÔ-SAMA IF I CAN KEEP HIM AT THE MANSION.

I'LL BE SURE TO LOCATE SOMEONE KIND TO ADOPT YOU.

I'M SORRY... FOR NOT BEING ABLE TO TAKE CARE OF YOU... I'M SORRY...

I KNOW, BUT...

...

Mew

SNIFF

JUST SO YOU KNOW, MARCH 3RD IS HINA-CHAN'S BIRTHDAY. ♡

SPARKLE

DRIP

HUH? OH, DON'T WORRY ABOUT THAT...

IS THERE ANYTHING I CAN DO FOR YOU?

BY THE WAY... I WANT TO REPAY THE FAVOR YOU DID IN ALLOWING ME TO STAY HERE FOR THREE DAYS AND TWO NIGHTS...

AH, SO MARCH 3RD IS HER BIRTHDAY.

WAH!! WHA...WHY ARE YOU BLURTING THAT OUT?!

YES. SO IF YOU WANT TO SHOW YOUR GRATITUDE, THIS COULD BE YOUR "BIG CHANCE"! ♡

PLUS YOU HAVE A RUNNY NOSE AND WATERY EYES FROM YOUR CAT ALLERGIES!!

WHA—?! WHAT CHANCE ?!

ALL RIGHT... IN THAT CASE, I'LL LOOK FORWARD TO RECEIVING IT.

SERIOUSLY... I'M TELLING YOU TO FORGET IT, BUT...

OKAY THEN, I'LL THINK OF A NICE PRESENT TO GIVE YOU.

YES!

WELL, THANKS AGAIN FOR YOUR HOSPITALITY!

...FOR BRINGING THIS KITTEN BACK WITH ME...

I WONDER IF I'M GOING TO GET SCOLDED...

URGH...

OH!! HAYATE'S BACK?

DING DONG

KLIK

WELL... NO SENSE WORRYING ABOUT IT NOW...

SORRY FOR MAKING YOU TAKE SOME TIME OFF ON MY...

WHST

HAYATE, WELCOME BACK!!

MEW?

...

...

IT'S BEEN A WHILE, OJÔ-SAMA.

AH.

STARE

...ACCOUNT...

120

UH... YES... THAT'S RIGHT...

YOU'VE BROUGHT BACK A KITTEN!!

HAYATE!! LOOK, YOU... THIS IS A KITTEN!! A KITTEN!!

Meow?

NOOOOOO!!

WHA-WHA-WHA-WHAT IS THAT, HAYATE?!

UH...I SUPPOSE THAT'S A NO?

KITTENS ARE NOT ALLOWED!!

THAT'S NOT ALLOWED, HAYATE!! NO KITTENS!!

AH, UMM... THIS IS...

Meow Meow?

...

...

NIBBLE NIBBLE

BA-DUMP BA-DUMP

BUT YOU JUST SAID...

UMM...

OF COURSE WE CAN KEEP HIM, HAYATE!!!

OKAY, FINE!!

EH?

I'LL RAISE HIM TO BE A FINE SANZENIN FAMILY CAT.

BUT DON'T WORRY.

STILL... THIS KITTEN TOOK ME BY SURPRISE, HAYATE.

YES. LEAVE IT TO ME.

PURR PURR

DO YOU MEAN YOU'RE KEEPING HIM AS A PET?

RAISE?

YES... I'M REALLY SORRY ...

...FOR THE CARE OF THIS LITTLE SNOWBALL OF A KITTEN, *SHIRANUI!!*

I WILL ACCEPT FULL RESPONSIBILITY...

HA HA HA, THAT'S NOT A PROBLEM EITHER.

BUT, I WONDER WHAT MARIA-SAN WILL SAY...

IT'S OKAY. THERE'S A PATCH OF WHITE RIGHT HERE, SO NO PROBLEM.

SNOW-BALL? BUT, HE'S A *BLACK* CAT...

WHO ARE YOU CALLING A *WITCH*?

WAIT A MINUTE!

EVER SINCE THE OLDEN DAYS, WITCHES AND BLACK CATS HAVE GONE TOGETHER.

A VERY *LARGE* ONE...

WE ALREADY HAVE A CAT...

HM? WHAT?

ANYWAY, IT'S NOT THAT I OBJECT, BUT HAVEN'T YOU FORGOTTEN SOMETHING?

DON'T WORRY, IT'S NOT LIKE I EAT KITTENS.

HA HA HA.

DO YOU KNOW HOW LONG OJÔ AND I HAVE BEEN TOGETHER?

BESIDES...

THAT'S BECAUSE I'M A GROWN-UP. I DON'T LET KIDS BOTHER ME.

HMM, YOU LOOK VERY COMPOSED.

HEY, TAMA—

...WHEN SHE'S LONESOME, I'M THE ONE WHO COMFORTS HER...

WHEN OJÔ CAN'T SLEEP, I'M THE ONE WHO CURLS UP BESIDE HER... AND EVEN NOW...

LISTEN, I HAVE SOMETHING TO TELL YOU.

MEOW!!

OH, TAMA, THERE YOU ARE.

...

SEE? JUST LIKE I SAID... BEING THE FAVORITE SURE KEEPS ME BUSY...

125

...WHO GETS IN THE WAY OF OUR RELATIONSHIP!!

I WON'T FORGIVE ANYONE (OR ANY CAT)...

I'VE ALWAYS BEEN OJÔ'S FAVORITE!!

OJÔ-SAMA, YOU SEEM TO BE VERY COMFORTABLE WITH CARING FOR THIS KITTEN.

...CLEANED THE LITTER BOX, PLAYED WITH HIM, SLEPT NEXT TO HIM...

I FED HIM MILK, GAVE HIM FOOD...

IT REALLY WAS DIFFICULT.

REALLY?

I WENT THROUGH A LOT OF HARD TIMES WITH TAMA BACK THEN.

...AND HAD HIM PLAY FF, DQ, VIRT◯A FIGHTER, TOHOU, THE KATATSUKI GAMES AND THE HIGURASHI GAMES, PLUS I MADE HIM GO BUY THE CUT A D◯SH!! FANZINE...

...SHOWED HIM THE ENTIRE GU◯DAM, E◯ANGELION, NADES◯CO, U◯NA, CY◯ER FORMULA, MAMAYON, GAOGA◯GAR AND ELDR◯N SERIES...

...

SO THAT'S WHY HE BECAME THAT KIND OF TIGER...

SERIOUSLY... THOSE WERE SOME HARD TIMES...

AHH...

YOU KNOW, EVEN AMONG HUMANS, A NEW BABY BROTHER OR SISTER TENDS TO MAKE THE OLDER SIBLINGS GRUMPY.

JEALOUS?

BUT... SPEAKING OF TAMA... HE SEEMS TO BE FEELING A BIT JEALOUS.

OH... A BATH.

I'M GOING TO TAKE A QUICK BATH.

HM?

HUH?

WHERE ARE YOU GOING, OJŌ-SAMA?

...HAYATE, COULD YOU LOOK AFTER SHIRANUI FOR A BIT?

WELL, I'LL PLAY WITH TAMA NEXT TIME, BUT FOR RIGHT NOW...

WHAT A HOPELESS GUY.

!!

BLUSH

SP...

YEAH... A BATH...

UH... RIGHT...

GEEZ!! JUST LOOK AFTER SHIRANUI, ALL *RIGHT*?!

SLAM

HUH?

WHY DID YOU HAVE TO REMIND ME ABOUT THAT?!

F-FOOL!!

THAT'S WHY... I CAME UP WITH *THIS* PLAN...

...HE'LL BE THE ONE TO GET KICKED OUT...

HE MUST KNOW THAT IF HE DOES ANY HARM TO SHIRANUI...

UNK UNK

BUT I WONDER WHAT TAMA IS GOING TO DO?

...

...AND CHASE HIM OUT OF HERE!!

SO I'VE GOT A PLAN THAT WILL MAKE OJÔ-SAMA *HATE* HIM...

HEH HEH HEH... I KNOW THERE'S NO POINT IN KILLING HIM.

WHAT KIND OF PLAN IS THIS?

TAMA... YOU...

TAK

I KNOW!!

HAH!!

WHAT WOULD MAKE OJÔ-SAMA NOT WANT TO KEEP SHIRANUI?

A PLAN... TO MAKE HER HATE THE KITTEN?

...AND PLACE THE BLAME ON HIM...

←Foot-print Stamps

BLACK INK

THE NOTEBOOK OJÔ-SAMA DRAWS HER MANGA IN...

THE NOTE-BOOK!!

THAT'S RIGHT... I'M GOING TO TEAR IT TO PIECES...

Manga Draft ⑥ "Magic

RRRIP RRRIP

I'LL NEVER ALLOW YOU TO...

GRR!! YOU COWARD!!

MEOW?! HOW COULD YOU ACTUALLY *DO* THAT?!

WAAH!! SHIRANUI!!

MEOWW...

IF...IF OJÔ-SAMA FINDS OUT...

CREAK

RRRIP RRRIP RRRIP RRRIP

...DO THAT...

MEW MEW MEW MEOW

JUST AS I PLANNED.

SNEER

...SHIRANUI BECAME NAGI'S PET.

ME-OOOOW!!

SHUT UP, TAMA!! REFLECT A LITTLE ON WHAT YOU'VE DONE!!

MEOW!! MEOW-MEOW!!

AND SO, THIS IS HOW...

SHE IS THE DESCENDANT OF A CLAN WHOSE OCCUPATION FOR GENERATIONS HAS BEEN SPECTER EXTERMINATION. IN THIS REGARD, IT IS GENERALLY AGREED UPON THAT SHE POSSESSES IMMENSE POWER.

ISUMI SAGINO-MIYA.

...SHE GOES. SHE LOSES HER WAY, BUT SHE KNOCKS IT DOWN.

Eeh
Eeh
Eeh
Eeh

IF SHE HEARS THERE'S A SPECTER IN THE WEST...

...SHE GOES. SHE TAKES A ROUNDABOUT PATH, BUT KNOCKS IT DOWN!

Eeh
Eeh
Eeh

IF SHE HEARS THERE'S AN EVIL SPIRIT IN THE EAST...

WITH A KILLING BLOW, SHE DRIVES AWAY EVIL SPIRITS!!

...SHE WILL RUSH TO THE SITE AND ALMOST MAKE IT IN TIME!!

...as last time... Umm.

It's the same pose...

IF YOU CALL HER TWO HOURS EARLIER, OR IF YOU CAN GIVE HER A DETAILED MAP AND A GUIDE...

134

...OF THE TORMENT AND SUFFERING... OF JUST SUCH A GIRL. (IMAGINE THIS BEING NARRATED BY TOMO◯WO TAGUCHI.)

THIS IS A TRUE STORY...

OH...

A KITTEN?

...HE'S REALLY TINY AND CUTE. ♡

HE'S A BLACK MALE KITTEN, BUT...

I SEE...

YEAH. HAYATE BROUGHT HIM HOME YESTERDAY. HE'S ABOUT A MONTH OLD.

WHAT ARE YOU SAYING? SURE, HE CAN BE A LITTLE MISCHIEVOUS, BUT HE'S STILL CUTE.

HMPF...

WELL... TAMA USED TO BE CUTE, TOO.

135

COME TO THINK OF IT, YOU DON'T WEAR THE SCHOOL UNIFORM, ISUMI-SAN...

WHY IS THAT?

T-THIS IS... UMM... I DON'T MEAN TO IGNORE THEM OR ANYTHING!!

CHANGE YOUR CLOTHES? EVEN THOUGH YOU'RE IGNORING SCHOOL REGULATIONS BY WEARING YOUR REGULAR CLOTHES ALREADY?

YES. I WILL GO HOME TO CHANGE MY CLOTHES, THEN COME OVER TO SEE YOU.

SIP

?

PANIC PANIC

EH? OH... TH-THAT'S... UM...

SO, SHE'S LIKE THE BRUTAL, LAW-BREAKING FIGHTER TYPE.

TO SUM UP, SHE JUST DOESN'T LIKE THE UNIFORM.

Ahh!!

I FEEL SHY ABOUT IT, SO...

WEARING A SKIRT FEELS TOO *BREEZY*...

YES, WE WILL BE WAITING FOR YOU TO ARRIVE...

...BY CAR.

I'LL BE WAITING FOR YOU TO ARRIVE BY CAR.

OKAY.

REGARD-LESS, I WILL VISIT YOUR PLACE LATER.

OH, ISUMI-SAN. WELCOME.

KA-CHAK

DING DONG

...SO I'M REALLY LOOKING FORWARD TO...

BUT I'VE NEVER SEEN ANY KITTENS EXCEPT TAMA...

BA-DUMP · BA-DUMP

ISUMI-SAN, DO YOU LIKE CATS, TOO?

YES.

SEE, THIS IS MY KITTEN, SHIRANUI.

OH, YOU'RE HERE!

NAGI... ISUMI-SAN'S HERE...

THIS LITTLE ONE IS...

OH...

138

...THE TROUBLE BEGAN!!

AND THEN ...

EH?

RRREOW

FSSSST!!

...TO ISUMI'S INNER POWER.

FSSST!!

SO HE OVER-REACTED...

KITTENS ARE VERY SENSITIVE AND TIMID CREATURES.

FSSST!!

H-HEY!! WHAT'S WRONG, SHIRANUI?!

PANIC PANIC

...AFFECTED HER DEEPLY. (AGAIN, IMAGINE THIS BEING NARRATED BY TOMO◯WO TAGUCHI.)

GLO——OM

EVEN THOUGH SHE POSSESSES GREAT POWER, SHE'S STILL ONLY 13 YEARS OLD. SO THIS SITUATION...

...I'D BE DISLIKED SO MUCH...

I DIDN'T THINK...

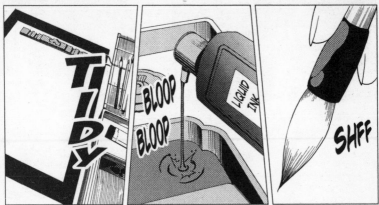

SHE'S TRYING TO WORK THROUGH HER EMOTIONS.

WHAT'S GOING ON THERE?

I HAVE TO CHANGE!!

IF YOU DON'T FIGHT, YOU CAN'T SURVIVE

*Catch phrase from *Masked Rider Ryuki*

I SHOULDN'T BE LIKE THIS.

...HOW TA BECOME A GIRL DAT CATS WILL LIKE?

SO... YA CAME HERE BECAUSE YA WANTED TA KNOW...

AIZAWA

DAT'S BECAUSE I USED TA WATCH ALL DA OLD *JARI○KO CHOE* RERUNS DAT WERE SHOWN IN DA KANSAI AREA!!

SURELY, NO ONE KNOWS MORE THAN I DO ABOUT HOW TA BE ADORED BY A CAT!!

I'D SAY YA MADE A GOOD DECISION.

HMM... DAT CHOICE YA MADE...

NOD NOD

SHE DOESN'T REALLY UNDERSTAND.

Nod Nod Nod

...

P-PLEASE DO.

I'LL TEACH YA HOW TA BE A GIRL THAT CATS *LOVE*!!

BUT DON'T WORRY!!

...DA FIRST THING YA USE IS SOME KONBU SEAWEED!!

WH ST

FIRST OF ALL, SINCE YER WEARIN' JAPANESE-STYLE CLOTHING...

LIGHT IT UP!!

FOOSH

THEN ...

WHST

HOLD IT IN YER RIGHT HAND...

CATS JUS' LOVE DRIED BONITO!!

AND YOU NEED A DRIED BONITO FISH, TOO!!

WRAP DAT AROUND YER HEAD!!

WRAPPED

BLAZE

SHISHIO'S FINAL SECRET MOVE. KAGUOCHI.

*Kuzu Ryusen

I WAS JUS' TEASING YA!!

S-sorry!!

W-WAIT!!

All you do is pick on me...

I WAS FOOLISH TO ASK YOU, SAKUYA...

B-BUT...

I'm too shy to wear modern clothes.

...SO DOESN'T IT MAKE SENSE TO START WITH JUS' CHANGIN' YER APPEARANCE?

DAY AFTER DAY YA WEAR A KIMONO... YA ALREADY KNOW KNOW YA CAN'T CHANGE WHO YA ARE THAT EASILY...

...DON'T YA THINK YA NEED TO CHANGE YER LOOK?

I WAS TEASIN' YA JUST NOW, BUT...

↰She smelled of Konbu seaweed, so she took a bath

143

TWITCH

!

BUT YA ARE *INTRIGUED* BY THEM, AREN'T YA?

TH-THAT'S...

DON'T YOU FEEL LIKE WEARING SOME FRILLY OUTFITS AT TIMES... LIKE WHAT NAGI WEARS?

Look here

ISUMI-SAN *IS* A GIRL, AFTER ALL...

MAYBE...

Mumble

...

AS I EXPECTED, IF DA GIRL LOOKS GOOD, SO DO DA CLOTHES...

WELL, WELL...

TEN MIN-UTES LATER...

YES! ♡

HELP OUR GUEST CHANGE HER CLOTHES!!

!!

WELL, DAT'S IT, THEN!! AIZAWA FAMILY MAIDS!!

SO YOU DRESSED UP IN ORDER TO BECOME A GIRL WHO'LL BE LIKED BY KITTENS...

OH...

...BUT THAT SKIRT SUITS YOU TOO, ISUMI-SAN. ♡

YOUR USUAL KIMONO IS CUTE, TOO...

RIGHT...

RIGHT, HAYATE?

YOU LOOK PRETTY CUTE.

...

...VERY MUCH...

THANK YOU...

AH...

!!

THAT'S TRUE—!!

WELL!! BUT IT'S NOT LIKE KITTENS CARE ABOUT THINGS LIKE THAT!!

NO! WAIT!! WAIT A MINUTE!!

...THAT THIS HAD BEEN A CASE OF THE TAIL WAGGING THE DOG...

...

THE GIRL FINALLY REALIZED...

PSSH

EH?

...IF THE KITTEN DISLIKES YOU THAT MUCH... WOULD YOU LIKE TO TRY A LITTLE MAGIC TRICK?

BUT ISUMI-SAN...

THIS IS A MILD SOLUTION OF MATATABI CATNIP EXTRACT. IT'S NOT GOOD TO SPRAY TOO MUCH OF IT, BUT...

...PERHAPS YOUR JAPANESE-STYLE CLOTHES HAD SOME KIND OF SCENT THAT CATS DISLIKE...

HAYATE-SAMA, WHAT'S...

Purr Purr

MEOW

WELL, HE IS AN **ANIMAL**, AFTER ALL...

...BECAUSE OF SOMETHING AS SIMPLE AS THAT?

I CAN BE LIKED OR DISLIKED...

Meow!

...

!!

IN SHORT, IT WAS ALL AN EMBARRASSIN' EXERCISE IN FUTILITY!!

Meow!?

LATER, CANDID PHOTOS OF THE GIRL IN HER MODERN CLOTHES WERE SOLD FOR 10,000 YEN* A PIECE...(TO THE LAST, IN THE NARRATION STYLE OF TOMO◯WO TAGUCHI.)

Well!

Whoa...

THAT'S FOR SURE.

THEY'RE REALLY GOOD FRIENDS, AREN'T THEY?

!!

Ahaha! Sorry, sorry!!

Mmf!!

Mmf!!

Episode 10:
"*Please Save My Earth*
With a 130cm Dandy, Darling

WELL THEN!!

NOW I'LL AVENGE MY FATHER'S DEATH!!

GUH

YOU WILL ALL...

WHO ARE YOU?

...SINCE THAT BATTLE!! VOOSH

ABOUT THREE WEEKS HAVE PASSED....

...THAT ARE SO FUNNY THEY'LL MAKE YOU FORGET ALL ABOUT REVENGE!

SPARKLE

IN RETURN, I'LL LOAN YOU SOME DVDS...

SPARKLE

TACHIBANA VIDEO RENTALS

...PUZZLED!!

SHE WAS...

SIGN-UP FREE CAMPAIGN

1 NIGHT 300 YEN UP

TACHIBANA VIDEO

SO... THERE'S NO NEED TO BE NERVOUS!!

BA-DUMP BA-DUMP

I'M JUST HERE TO RENT A DVD...

A DVD...

...RUNS COMPLETELY COUNTER TO COMMON SENSE...

AFTER ALL, FALLING IN LOVE WITH A 13-YEAR-OLD BOY...

WHY?

BUT SHE HADN'T SEEN HIM SINCE...

THREE WEEKS HAD PASSED SINCE THAT BATTLE.

BUT HE'S ONLY 13!! THE MORE TIME PASSED, GIVING HER A CHANCE TO CALMLY THINK IT OVER, THE MORE SHE REALIZED IT WASN'T A GOOD THING!! IT'S A CRIME!! PLUS, SHE'S A NUN!!

BUT... I'M STILL FEELING WEAK...

YOU... YOU CAN UNDER- STAND... HOW I...

HIS PLEASANT SMILE MADE HER FALL IN LOVE ON THE SPOT!!

THE ART BAD IONS SUCCEED V YOU AVE ENT EVIL?

TCH. WHO SAID I NEED YOUR HELP...?

BUT IT WAS LOVE AT FIRST SIGHT!!

THAT'S RIGHT!! MAYBE I'M MISTAKEN!! AFTER ALL, HOW COULD I POSSIBLY FALL IN LOVE WITH A YOUNG BOY LIKE THAT?!

...IF THIS FEELING IS REAL...

I DIDN'T COME HERE TO SEE THE BOY I LOVE... I CAME HERE TO CONFIRM...

YES... I SHOULD CHANGE THE WAY I THINK ABOUT THIS.

WSSST

OKAY, THEN!!

CLENCH

Ngh...

UH... OH? SISTER?

WELCOME.

SO... I JUST... I JUST STOPPED BY TO RENT IT FROM YOU...

Rent

I JUST REMEMBERED THAT YOU SAID YOU'D LOAN ME A DVD.

TH-THAT'S REALLY NONE OF YOUR BUSINESS.

HOW HAVE YOU BEEN?

I HAVEN'T SEEN YOU IN A WHILE...

...SINCE YOU'RE JUST A KID...

WELL... YOU MIGHT HAVE FORGOTTEN SUCH A PROMISE...

EH?

...I WENT AHEAD AND PICKED OUT SOME OF MY FAVORITES.

SINCE YOU DIDN'T SHOW UP AFTER THAT...

!!

PLOP PLOP PLOP PLOP

WHO ELSE IS THERE?

FOR... ME?

BLUSH

...

WHAT DO YOU THINK?

I RECOMMEND THIS ONE...

BIG SMILE

YOU'RE RECOMMENDING ANIME TO ME?

ISN'T THIS ANIME?

HMPH... Y-YOU'RE JUST A CHILD AFTER ALL...

BA-DUMP BA-DUMP

WHAT'S WITH THAT SMILE?!

WHA...

...I'LL GIVE IT A TRY...

WELL, JUST FOR THE HECK OF IT...

NO FAIR USING THAT SMILE OF YOURS ON ME!!

SMILE

WELL, JUST TRUST ME AND WATCH IT!!

KYA!!

CRASH

2 DAYS 3 NIGHTS

UH... UMM...

IF THAT'S THE CASE, I MIGHT AS WELL CONFESS MY FEELINGS...

NOT GOOD...NO MISTAKE ABOUT IT, I SEEM TO HAVE FALLEN IN LOVE WITH THIS BOY...

YEAH. LET ME KNOW WHAT YOU THINK AFTER YOU WATCH THEM.

154

...

OWWW...

!

TP

HEY!! SAKI, ARE YOU ALL RIGHT?!

...

SERIOUSLY... IF YOU'RE NOT CAREFUL, YOU'RE REALLY GOING TO KILL YOURSELF SOMEDAY.

S-SORRY...

...

OH... I'M ALL RIGHT...

YOU FOOL! NEVER MIND THAT. DID YOU GET HURT? HUH?

I'M SORRY, I BUMPED INTO THE SHELF AGAIN...

155

WHO IS SHE? THAT WOMAN...

...PLEASE STOP CHOKING ME...

...I only came here to return some DVDs...

CLENCH

UM...

B-BUT, BEFORE I EXPLAIN...

SHE'S VERY DEAR TO WATARU-KUN...

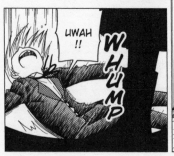

UWAH!!

WHUMP

UM... WELL, SHE IS... UM...

GOD SAYS THAT I CAN ONLY PUT YOU DOWN IF YOU TELL ME WHO SHE IS FIRST.

DANGLE

...THAT THERE WAS ANY SUCH WOMAN...

I DIDN'T KNOW...

UH... SISTER?

Hello?

...TO WATARU-KUN...!

A DEAR PERSON...

!!

PLIP

YEAH, BUT... BRO...

ARE YOU READY?

DID... DID I DO THAT?! WHAT DID I DO?!

WHOA!! WHOA!!

VIDEO

SO THERE'S A RICH GUY AT THIS VIDEO SHOP?

THAT'S RIGHT.

I DIDN'T PLAN OUT THE PREVIOUS KIDNAPPING. SO I DID SOME THOROUGH RESEARCH THIS TIME.

YOU FOOL. I'VE LOOKED INTO IT.

WHY DO YOU WANT TO KIDNAP SOMEONE AGAIN? AND NOT ONLY THAT, WHY A KID FROM SOME VIDEO SHOP?

YOU FINALLY ESCAPED FROM PRISON...

YOUR BRAIN IS LIKE A SUPER-COMPUTER!!

I SEE!! NO ONE POOR HAS A MAID!! THAT'S MY BRO!!

AFTER ALL, THERE'S A *MAID* AT THIS VIDEO SHOP!!

...

UM...

HUH?

WELL, I JUST WALKED STRAIGHT IN AND KIDNAPPED HER!!

S-SORRY !!

YOU FOOL!! WHAT'S THE POINT IN KID-NAPPING THE MAID?!

FWIP

158

SAKI!!

EHH?! S-SOMEONE PLEASE HELP ME!!

WHATEVER!! NOW THAT IT'S COME TO THIS, WE MAY AS WELL JUST KIDNAP HER ANYWAY!!

HUH?

IS THIS *DIVINE INTERVENTION?*

...

UWAH!! W-WE'VE GOT TROUBLE, SISTER!!

WHAT ARE YOU SAYING?

GOD JUST ELIMINATED THAT NUISANCE FOR ME...

...

G-GOT IT!!

WATARU-KUN, GO CALL THE POLICE!!

I'LL GO AFTER THE CAR!!

...THAT MAID?

ARE YOU IN LOVE WITH...

HM?

HEY.

SKRITCH

IN THAT CASE...

SO IN THAT SENSE, SHE'S VERY DEAR TO ME...ANYWAY, NONE OF THAT MATTERS RIGHT NOW...

HUH?! FOO...!! WHAT ARE YOU SAYING?! S-SAKI IS LIKE *FAMILY* TO ME...

!!

WOULD YOU RISK YOUR LIFE... FOR HER SAKE?

...

WELL?

I SEE...

WELL THEN...

WHAT WOULD YOU EXPECT?!

OF COURSE...

SMAK

!

!!

NOW YOU **HAVE** TO RESCUE HER!!

THAT WAS AN **ADVANCE** !!

...

WHA...?

...

BLAZE

BLAZE

...THE CAR AND THE GANGSTERS WERE BOTH WRECKED...

GANGSTERS

BLAZE

BY THE TIME I CAUGHT UP WITH THEM...

...

BLAZE BLAZE AND SAKI-SAN HAD BEEN RESCUED UNHARMED.

...WAS PRETTY INTERESTING.

THIS ANIME...

GLAD TO HEAR IT.

IS THAT SO?

OH...

SAKI-SAN, IS ANYTHING WRONG?

NO... I DON'T KNOW WHY, BUT...

WELL? SO WHAT'S NEXT?

NEXT... LET'S SEE...

...

SIZZLE

AND THIS IS HOW...

WAKA, IS THERE SOMETHING YOU'RE HIDING FROM ME?

URGH... EH?! NO!! I'M NOT HIDING ANYTHING!!

...A BOY TAKES A STEP TOWARDS BECOMING A MAN.

Urgh...

...WHEN I SEE THOSE TWO TALKING...

...I FEEL SOMETHING LIKE *MURDEROUS INTENT* RISING...

OH...

TACHIBANA VIDEO

Episode 11:
"I Used to Think That It Was Normal to Fish Like the Crazy Old Men of the Sea"

I'M BORED...

THERE'S NO TWO WAYS ABOUT IT...

IT'S THE SCHOOL THAT BORES ME.

NOW THAT YOU'RE ALLOWED TO COME HOME EARLY BEFORE THE TESTS BEGIN...

BUT YOU JUST GOT HOME FROM SCHOOL. WHAT'S WRONG?

YOU SHOULDN'T CONFUSE ANIME WITH *REALITY*.

HAYATE.

IF YOU'RE THAT BORED, WHY DON'T YOU START UP AN SOS BRIG◯?

Sigh

GAH!!
I never expected to hear that from ojō-sama...

PLEASE SAVE THAT COMPLAINT FOR WHEN YOU ACTUALLY GO TO SCHOOL EVERY DAY.

I CAN'T HELP BUT BE BORED.

IT'S THE SAME THING, DAY AFTER DAY.

FWUMP

TRY STUDYING!!

...READ SOME MANGA.

...I GUESS I'LL...

TO KILL THIS BOREDOM...

EH?

...

I AGREE...

WHEN OJŌ-SAMA READS MANGA... SHE GETS SO QUIET...

...OJŌ-SAMA'S READING MANGA INSTEAD OF STUDYING...

BUT...

BLURP BLURP

BAM

BUT WHEN SHE'S FINISHED, SHE'S USUALLY...

LET'S GO FISHING!!

HAYATE!!

...INFLUENCED BY THE STORY...

...

HUH?

LAKE SANZENIN?

REALLY...

That's small?

YES!! BUT IT'S REALLY JUST A SMALL LAKE, ONLY ABOUT *1.25 MILES* IN DIAMETER.

YOU MEAN THIS MANSION HAS A LAKE TOO?

RIGHT. IT'S ON THE GROUNDS OF THE MANSION, BUT IT'S PRETTY DECENT.

EH?

BUT EVEN THOUGH YOU SAID IT'S BIG ENOUGH, CAN WE REALLY FISH IN A LAKE THAT'S ON THE GROUNDS OF THE MANSION?

AH, MARIA-SAN.

YES, YOU CAN.

...SO THE LAKE IS ALMOST LIKE ITS OWN GALAXY...

HER GRANDFATHER RELEASED VARIOUS FISH FROM ALL OVER THE WORLD INTO IT, WHICH CREATED THEIR OWN UNIQUE ECOSYSTEM...

...AND ITS SOURCE IS A NATURAL SPRING, SO THE WATER IS PURE...

THE PUBLIC CAN'T GET TO IT SINCE IT'S ON PRIVATE PROPERTY...

IT'S A VERY CONVENIENT THING TO HAVE AROUND.

THE DAY'S CATCH MAKES IT EASY TO DETERMINE THE DINNER MENU...

OF COURSE, I BUY SALT-WATER FISH FROM THE MARKET. ♡

SO, THE FISH SERVED IN THIS HOUSE ARE SELF-SUSTAINED!!

EH? DOES THAT MEAN THAT WHILE WE'RE AT SCHOOL, MARIA-SAN GOES FISHING?!

RIGHT!! LET'S GO, HAYATE!!

W-WELL, NOW THAT WE KNOW WE CAN REALLY FISH...WHY DON'T WE HEAD OVER THERE...

SANZENIN FAMILY PRIVATE FOREST

LAKE SANZENIN

ANNEX

RIDING GROUNDS

OHHH!! THIS IS QUITE A LAKE, ISN'T IT?!

...BEGINS WITH CRUCIAN CARP AND ENDS WITH CRUCIAN CARP!!

CRUCIAN CARP = HERA CRUCIAN

FISHING...

EH?

SHK

WELL, THEN HOW ABOUT A *DOUGH BALL* INSTEAD OF AN EARTHWORM?

WHAT YOU SAID MAKES ME WONDER IF THE SANZENIN FAMILY IS REALLY THAT AMAZING OR NOT.

YES. FOR THE FIRST TIME IN MANY YEARS, I'D LIKE TO ENJOY FISHING FOR CRUCIAN CARP WITHOUT WORRYING ABOUT CATCHING IT FOR FOOD.

AH... MARIA-SAN, ARE YOU GOING TO FISH, TOO?

AH, YES.

HMPH. ANYWAY, HAYATE, LET'S PREPARE TO GO FLY-FISHING!!

I'LL TEACH YOU THAT REAL FISHING HAS NOTHING TO DO WITH LOOKING COOL.

...THAT KIND OF FISHING DOESN'T LOOK VERY COOL...

BUT...

I ROUGHLY UNDERSTAND HOW TO USE THE EQUIPMENT.

ALL RIGHT!!

OKAY. THEN I'LL JUST ADJUST THE LURE ACCORDINGLY...

MEANWHILE, I'M GOING TO CATCH THE *LORD OF THIS LAKE!!*

Heh heh heh ...

WELL, HAYATE, YOU JUST WORK AT CATCHING SOME LITTLE FISHY OVER THERE.

...I'LL HAVE TO BE CAREFUL THAT OJÔ-SAMA DOESN'T HURT HERSELF AND GET TANGLED IN THE LINES...

BUT I CAN ALMOST SEE WHAT'S COMING NEXT, SO...

IT'S DANGEROUS IF YOU DON'T HOLD IT TIGHTLY.

Ooh?

HAYATE. MY FISHING ROD FLEW AWAY.

...

EH?

Whoop?

SPLASH

!!

WOW!! MARIA-SAN, YOU ALREADY...

THIS CRUCIAN HAS A PRETTY NICE SHAPE.

HMM.

TUG

EH?!

SHWUP

AH!! I THINK I'VE GOT SOMETHING, TOO.

A-ALL RIGHT, THEN!! THEN I WILL TOO!!

OH!! IS THAT RIGHT?! REALLY?!

UWAAH... OJÔ-SAMA!! I CAN CATCH A TON OF FISH IN THIS LAKE.

SHWUP

SWIP

WHOOP

Aah...

SHWUP

SWIP

WHOOP

Aah...

BECAUSE MY FISHING RODS KEPT FLYING AWAY!!

YOU GOT TIRED OF IT SO FAST.

BECAUSE YOU DON'T HOLD THEM TIGHT ENOUGH.

...BORING...

FISHING IS...

GRRR

...MAYBE IT'S BETTER TO FISH OFFSHORE IN A BOAT.

BUT IF YOUR ROD KEEPS FLYING AWAY, THEN...

BUT IT'S EXTREMELY DIFFICULT TO GO FLY-FISHING ON A BOAT...

HUH? A BOAT?

SO, GO GET THE BOAT, HAYATE.

WELL... IT CAN'T BE HELPED. I WILL GIVE UP FLY-FISHING FOR YOU...

?

...

175

S-SHUT UP!! JUST GO PREPARE THE BOAT!!

EH? WHY DID YOU SUDDENLY...

OKAY? YOU HOLD THE REEL LIKE THIS AND...

...AS SOON AS HE WAS ALONE WITH ME ON THIS BOAT, HE STARTED GETTING SO CLOSE... HE'S UN-EXPECTEDLY DARING...

B-BUT, THAT HAYATE...

THIS WAY, YOU CAN CAST THE LINE PROPERLY, RIGHT?

OH? YEAH...

BUT OJÔ-SAMA IS SO TINY... I FEEL LIKE I'M HOLDING A KITTEN...

IF SHE WHIPS THE FISHING ROD AROUND ON THE BOAT, SHE'LL FALL IN FOR SURE, SO I HAVE TO HOLD HER STEADY...

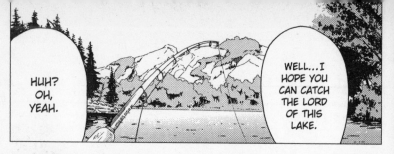

HUH? OH, YEAH.

WELL... I HOPE YOU CAN CATCH THE LORD OF THIS LAKE.

EH?!

AH!! OJÔ-SAMA, YOU'VE GOT SOMETHING!!

TUG

HUH?

WELL... I WON'T MIND IF I DON'T CATCH ANYTHING.

I DON'T KNOW, BUT IT'S PRETTY...

DO YOU THINK IT'S THE LORD OF THE LAKE?!

...

...Oh-oh...

SPLISH

...BIG?

WATCH OUT, OJÔ-SAMA!!

WAH!!

Y A N K

!!

THE ONE WHO NEEDS TO LET GO IS *YOU*!!

OJÔ-SAMA, LET GO OF THE ROD!!

UWAA, HAYATE!! LOOK, YOU...!! WATCH WHAT YOU'RE GRABBING!!

NGH!!

F-FOOL!! IF YOU HOLD ME THAT TIGHTLY—

OJÔ-SAMA, IF YOU DON'T LET GO OF THE ROD QUICKLY, THEN—

AH!!

SNAP

GLARE

OJÔ-SAMA, YOU'RE PRETTY *SMALL*...

BUT YOU SHOULDN'T PUSH YOURSELF SO HARD.

WHEW, AREN'T YOU GLAD, OJÔ-SAMA...

...THAT THE LINE BROKE?

BLOOSH

WELL, THE ONE THAT GOT AWAY IS ALWAYS THE LARGEST...

BUT, YOU CAME PRETTY CLOSE.

EH? EH? WH-WHAT ARE YOU TALKING ABOUT?

SHUT UP!! HINAGIKU'S ARE ABOUT THE SAME SIZE!!

WELL, LET'S GET MARIA-SAN AND GO HO—

WHEW

FLOP FLOP

POK POK

...

...

JUST AS I SAID.

THAT'S CLASSIFIED INFORMATION. ♡

THERE'S NOTHING A MAID CAN'T DO.

SO? HOW DID YOU CATCH IT?

FISHING BEGINS WITH CRUCIAN CARP AND ENDS WITH CRUCIAN CARP...

... YOU'RE RIGHT.

SINCE THEY COULDN'T EAT IT, THEY RELEASED IT.

TO BE CONTINUED

HAYATE THE COMBAT BUTLER

BONUS PAGES

I'M GOING TO DISREGARD BLUE AND BLACK TODAY AND DO THIS ALONE.♡ PLEASE LEND ME YOUR SUPPORT.♡

HELLO, HELLO!♡ SO HOW DID YOU LIKE VOL. 8? AS "RED RANGER, PRESIDENT OF THE CLASS" IZUMI SEGAWA, I'M IN CHARGE OF THE END OF THIS BOOK.♡

THIS IS TRULY A PERFECT PROJECT FOR THE EXPERT MASTER HOST "RED, PRESIDENT OF THE CLASS."♡

 Amazing!! A Super☆ Special Idea.♡

THIS PROJECT'S OBJECTIVE IS TO INTRODUCE THE STAFF WHO HAVE BEEN AIDING IN THE PRODUCTION OF THIS MANGA!!

THE HAYATE THE COMBAT BULTER STAFF INTERVIEW! ♡

NOW ON TO OUR END-OF-BOOK PROJECT !!

 ...NOTHING SPECIAL...

UM, SO YOU'RE ASKING ME HOW I LIKE MY WORK, BUT IT'S...

HUH?

HOW DO YOU LIKE YOUR WORK?!

WELL, LET'S GET STARTED.♡ FIRST UP, STAFF MEMBER G!!

ANYTHING INTERESTING GOING ON IN YOUR LIFE LATELY?

NOTHING SPECIAL...

WHAT DO YOU THINK OF THE AUTHOR?

NOTHING SPECIAL...

OKAY, OKAY. WELL, IS YOUR WORK DEMANDING?

NOTHING SPECIAL...

YIKES!! RED, PRESIDENT OF THE CLASS, IS IN DEEP TROUBLE. WH-WHAT SHOULD I DO?!

This project is failing from the start...

OH NO!! WHEN THE AUTHOR IS SHY AND WITHDRAWN, HIS STAFF TENDS TO BE THE SAME WAY!!

STRIP NAKED!!!

B-BUT WHAT POWER? WHAT AM I SUPPOSED TO DO, BLUE?!

AH!! THAT'S BLUE'S VOICE!!

DOOOM

AT A THE TIME LIKE THIS, YOU SHOULD USE YOUR *POWER!!*

WELL, SEE YOU IN VOLUME 9! ♡

Black here. That's all for now. ~♥

Aloha ♥ Catch me if you can.

I'll become a thug.

GEEZ!! DON'T SAY THAT!!

SO NOW'S THE TIME TO USE IT!!

Amazingly, you've gotten a great response from the readers!!!

YOU'RE THE TYPE WHO LOVES TO BE BULLIED, STRANGE GIRL RED!!

...

PROFILE

[Age]
About one month?

[Birthday]
Considering the day
he was found,
about January 20th?

[Blood Type]
?

[Height]
Really small

[Weight]
Really light

[Strengths/Likes]
Maria, Nagi, Milk

[Weaknesses/Dislikes]
Tigers

Shiranui

There already was a plan for his appearance
about the time Tama appeared in the story,
and the editor and I were talking about doing
an episode where Tama goes berserk after
Nagi brings home a stray kitten.
The punch line is somewhat of a parody, though.
The cat's personality, name and so on were
improvised, and although the name arose
from a video game that I was into at that time,
I didn't realize that until after I'd named it.
Kittens are difficult to draw, so I'm drawing
him like a miniature version of a mature cat.
In reality, a real kitten that's about a month
old is smaller and insanely cute.
Whenever I saw our own grown-up cat,
I would think I'd been deceived,
but when she nestles up to me,
I think she's the cutest cat in the universe.
Yes, I'm a doting father.
By the way, my cat is not black.

HI!
SO NOW THAT YOU'VE READ "*HAYATE THE COMBAT BUTLER*" VOLUME 8, HOW DID YOU LIKE IT?

THIS BOOK WAS ORGANIZED A LITTLE DIFFERENTLY FROM USUAL IN ORDER TO PLACE BONUS EPISODE #2—WHICH I WROTE DURING GOLDEN WEEK THIS YEAR—AT THE VERY END.

BONUS EPISODE #2 IS SIMILAR TO THE PREVIOUS BONUS EPISODE IN THAT IT'S A STORY THAT TAKES PLACE DURING THE MANGA'S GOLDEN WEEK TIME FRAME. IT'S THE STORY OF HINAGIKU'S AND NISHIZAWA-SAN'S TRIP TO TURKEY AND ATHENS. WHY DID I CHOOSE SUCH A SETTING? I HOPE I CAN TELL YOU SOMEDAY.

THIS MANGA SERIES IS FINALLY ABOUT TO HAVE ITS TWO-YEAR ANNIVERSARY, AND THE 100TH EPISODE IS DUE TO APPEAR IN THE MAGAZINE IT'S SERIALIZED IN SOON.

THANK YOU VERY MUCH. I CAN'T THANK YOU ENOUGH! YOUR SUPPORT MADE ALL OF THIS POSSIBLE! I REALLY WANT TO EXPRESS MY SINCERE THANKS AND APPRECIATION.

SO MANY THINGS HAPPEN IN LIFE, BUT I WILL RALLY MYSELF TO WORK EVEN HARDER, SO PLEASE LOOK FORWARD TO THE NEXT VOLUME.

I UPDATE WEB SUNDAY EVERY WEEK AS USUAL, SO PLEASE TAKE A LOOK AT THE SITE.
HTTP://WEBSUNDAY.NET
WELL, UNTIL THE TIME WE MEET AGAIN... BYE FOR NOW!

"Small Two of Pieces"

SO THIS IS CAPPA-DOCIA!!

UWAAH—!!

WOW... PEOPLE USED TO *LIVE* INSIDE THOSE ROCKS!!

HELLO, I'M AYUMU NISHIZAWA!! TODAY IS APRIL 29TH. DURING THE GOLDEN WEEK HOLIDAYS, WE WENT TO CAPPADOCIA IN TURKEY.

THEY'RE LIKE CAMEL'S HUMPS...

HEEEY! LOOK, LOOK, HINA-SAN!!

THAT'S A REAL CAMEL.

WOW. YES, THEY REALLY *DO* LOOK LIKE CAMEL'S HUMPS...

...YOU WERE STILL ABLE TO BOARD AN AIRCRAFT...

BUT EVEN THOUGH YOU SAID YOU DON'T LIKE HIGH PLACES...

AYUMU, YOU ALREADY KNOW THAT I DON'T LIKE HIGH PLACES!!

NO!! I DON'T NEED TO!!

COME ON, YOU CAN'T SEE THE VIEW UNLESS YOU'RE HIGHER UP...

GEEZ, YOU'RE ALWAYS JOKING AROUND.

GEEZ, I GUESS THERE'S NO OTHER CHOICE...

AT ANY RATE, I'M GOING TO ENJOY THE VIEW FROM A LOWER VANTAGE POINT!!

COME TO THINK OF IT, YOU DIDN'T EAT ANY IN-FLIGHT MEALS...

And the trip took 13 hours...

NO MATTER WHAT, I REFUSED TO WAKE UP UNTIL IT LANDED!!

THAT'S WHY I WAS FAST ASLEEP BEFORE WE TOOK OFF!!

SO THIS IS *ATHENS*!!

UWAAAH—!!

I THINK THIS VIEW IS TRULY PART OF OUR WORLD HERITAGE...

IT'S AMAZING!! FROM THE PARTHENON, YOU CAN SEE THE ENTIRE CITY.

THAT'S OKAY!! I SAID I DON'T NEED TO!! I DON'T NEED TO LOOK AT VIEWS FROM HIGH PLACES!!

OH, THERE YOU GO AGAIN. WELL, IT'S YOUR LOSS MISSING OUT ON THIS VIEW...

THIS TEMPLE IS WHAT'S PART OF OUR WORLD HERITAGE. THE VIEW HAS NOTHING TO DO WITH IT.

...SO WHY IS HINA-SAN STARING AT THE TEMPLE WITH SINGLE-MINDED DEVOTION?

BOURGEOIS KIDS...

THE THREE OF THEM SAID, "WE SAW ENOUGH OF THIS BACK IN KINDERGARTEN"...

IF SIGHTSEEING IS WHAT YOU WANTED, YOU SHOULD'VE BROUGHT THEM ALONG!!

FOR THAT MATTER, WHERE ARE MIKI AND THE OTHERS?!

SO WHY ARE YOU STILL SO ENERGETIC?

NOW THAT YOU MENTION IT, AYUMU, YOU WERE INVOLVED IN THAT RUCKUS, TOO.

PLUS, THEY RAISED A RUCKUS YESTERDAY, SO THEY WANTED TO SLEEP IN AT THE HOTEL UNTIL IT WAS TIME TO GET ON THE SHIP TO MYKONOS...

...

ISN'T THIS A TRIP TO DEEPEN OUR FRIENDSHIP?

OH, THAT'S BECAUSE THIS IS MY FIRST TRIP WITH HINA-SAN.

OKAY, OKAY. ♡

JUST DON'T LET GO OF MY *HAND*, ALL RIGHT?! PROMISE?!

UMM, THE VIEW IS OVER HERE...

HUH? OH!!

WELL?

SO WHERE CAN WE SEE THIS BEAUTIFUL VIEW YOU WERE TELLING ME ABOUT?

The End

A Person Who Sees Through

SEGAWA-SAN, WHY DID YOU DECIDE TO BECOME CLASS PRESIDENT?

BECAUSE WHEN THE CLASS COMMITTEE MEMBERS WERE BEING ELECTED, KATSURA-CHAN SAID...

YOU MUST BE CLASS PRESIDENT!!

IF THE CLASS PRESIDENT IS MORE COMPETENT THEN I AM, IT'LL MAKE ME LOOK BAD!!

THAT'S A TERRIBLE STORY...

OH NO, IT'S NOT THAT BAD.

FOR YUKIJI TO SEE THAT IN YOU AT A GLANCE...

WHAT DO YOU MEAN BY THAT, HAYATA-KUN?

A Person Who Can See

FATHER, MOST PEOPLE CAN'T SEE YOU ANYMORE, RIGHT?

YES. INCLUDING YOURSELF, THERE'RE PROBABLY ONLY FOUR OR FIVE PEOPLE WHO CAN SEE ME.

Like peeping on Maria-san when she's changing...

HA, DON'T BE SILLY. I'M A SERVANT OF GOD.

IF SO, I HOPE YOU AREN'T TAKING ADVANTAGE OF YOUR INVISIBILITY TO DO ANYTHING NAUGHTY.

THE ROAD TO GOD IS LONG AND RUGGED. BUT CONQUERING IT MAKES IT ALL WORTHWHILE.

BESIDES, I'M NOT PEEKING, I'M MERELY WITNESSING WHAT IS REVEALED TO ME, BOY!!

TH-THIS GUY IS TROUBLE...

I NEED TO DO SOME-THING ABOUT HIM SOON...